LEONARDO BOFF

THE PATH TO HOPE

Fragments from a Theologian's Journey

Translated by Phillip Berryman

Photographs by Mev Puleo

ORBIS BOOKS

Maryknoll, New York 10545

The Catholic Foreign Mission Society of America (Maryknoll) recruits and trains people for overseas missionary service. Through Orbis Books Maryknoll aims to foster the international dialogue that is essential to mission. The books published, however, reflect the opinions of their authors and are not meant to represent the official position of the society.

ORBIS/ISBN 0-88344-815-7

Contents

Editor's Note

In 1991 friends and admirers of the Brazilian theologian Leonardo Boff published two thin volumes of extracts from his works. Their aim was both to honor Boff at a time when he was under pressure and to offer the public, primarily familiar with his reputation for controversy, a selection representing the breadth and spiritual depth of his work. From the sixty-five books he had written or co-authored, along with innumerable articles and interviews, they gathered several hundred extracts and then organized them thematically. Boff himself was not involved in the selection and editing process. This English translation combines the two original volumes plus additional texts selected from available English translations. Many of the original selections have been omitted, and the order has been slightly rearranged.

As this volume was being prepared for publication Boff publicly announced his decision to leave the priesthood as well as his Franciscan community. In a letter addressed to his "Companions on the Path of Hope" (added to this volume) he described the sequence of external pressures that had made it increasingly difficult for him to continue his work as a theologian. As he wrote, "To be unfaithful to what gives sense to one's life is to lose one's dignity and to diminish one's identity. This I will not do, nor do I think that God wants this of us."

Boff's announcement surrounds the publication of this book with a weight unanticipated by the original editors. While not his last contribution as a theologian, this collection does represent a turning point in Boff's journey, as well as a significant vantage point from which to evaluate his considerable contributions to the church.

Born in Concordia Brazil in 1938, the eldest of eleven children, Boff entered the Franciscan order and was later ordained a priest in 1964. He earned his doctorate in theology in Munich in 1971. Returning to Brazil, he soon established himself as a prolific and influential theologian, publishing on such far-ranging topics as eschatology, christology, ecclesiology, and grace, as well as popular works on spirituality. In the early 1970s, beginning with his book *Jesus Christ Liberator*, he began to adopt the perspective of the emerging theology of liberation, surveying all questions of faith from the standpoint of the poor and oppressed. Through his many books, his work with the Brazilian bishops and the wider Latin American church, Boff emerged as one of the leading representatives of liberation theology, and, indeed, as one of the most prominent theologians of the world church.

In 1981 he published *Church: Charism and Power*, a collection of essays that applied the critique of liberation theology to the exercise of authority and power in the institutional church. He was subsequently summoned to Rome as part of a well-publicized investigation by the Congregation for the Doctrine of the Faith. In 1985 he was ordered to maintain a period of silence, which lasted eleven months. In explaining his willingness to submit to this discipline, Boff stated, "I would rather walk with the church than walk alone with my theology." However, Boff's tensions with church authorities continued over the next decade, culminating finally in his announcement of June 26, 1992.

In resigning from the priesthood Boff took pains to stress that he was not leaving the church or abandoning his vocation as a theologian: "I continue to be and will always be a theologian in the Catholic and ecumenical mold, fighting with the poor against their poverty and in favor of their liberation."

The selections which follow reflect one theologian's journey on the path to hope. Readers may judge whether the struggle has, in Boff's words, been "worth it." What shines through is Boff's Franciscan sensitivity, his impatience with injustice, and his very Catholic sacramental imagination. If there is a central theme it is perhaps the Kingdom of God, a reality already present in our midst, while at the same time remaining in its fullness on the horizon, beckoning and challenging us to continue the journey.

Sources

Newspapers and magazines are identified by name; books are indicated with initials. Full titles of books are found in the complete listing of books written or co-written by Boff at the end of this volume.

AM	*A Ave-Maria: O Feminino e o Espírito Santo*
CCP	*Church: Charism and Power*
CPCH	*Como Pregar a Cruz Hoje numa Sociedade de Crucificados*
DHM	*O Destino do Homem e do Mundo*
EHJ	*Encarnação: A Humanidade e a Jovialidade de Nosso Deus*
FA	*Francisco de Assis*
FB	*O Que Ficou: Balanço aos 50*
FE	*Faith on the Edge*
IFP	*E a Igreja se Fez Povo*
JCL	*Jesus Christ Liberator*
LG	*Liberating Grace*
LP	*The Lord's Prayer*
PCPW	*Passion of Christ, Passion of the World*
RCNR	*A Ressurreição de Cristo — A Nossa Ressurreição na Morte*
SAL	*Salvation and Liberation*
SF	*Saint Francis*
SL	*Sacraments of Life, Life of the Sacraments*
STMC	*Santíssima Trindade é a Melhor Comunidade*
TCL	*Teología de Cautiverio y Libertade*

TEP	*Teologia à Escuta do Povo*
TS	*Trinity and Society*
VAM	*Vida para Além da Morte*
VSE	*Vida Segundo o Espírito*
VSR	*Via-Sacra da Resurreição*
WTLP	*When Theology Listens to the Poor*

Autobiographical Notes

I am a descendant of Italian immigrants. At the turn of the century, my grandparents came to Guaporé in the state of Rio Grande do Sul, and from there my parents went to Concórdia, Santa Catarina. My brothers and sisters have headed out to Curibita, Paraná, and even to Mato Grosso do Sul. In other words, the reasons they left Italy amid an industrial boom are still present in Brazil. Our industrial system continues to expel those who are regarded as surplus — back then in Italy, and today in Brazil. It is always creating victims. Although this has been my family experience, I still regard myself as privileged. My ten brothers and sisters and I have all studied at university, and five of us have done graduate work overseas.

The most influential person in my life was my father. He had had a Jesuit education. After leaving the seminary, he went out into the wilds of Santa Catarina and served as teacher, druggist, accountant, and a much sought after advisor to the people. He helped Italian and German immigrants, who had to fend for themselves. Even back in the 1940s, he had his own literacy program, teaching everybody — children and adults, who spoke only Italian or German — to read and write. I spoke hardly anything but Italian myself until I was ten. My father used the radio to teach Portuguese, and he got people together in meetings after Sunday prayer.

In his view, life meant serving the community. He was a very ethical person, and was friendly to the mulattos, who

suffered discrimination there. He died in the middle of his
work, when he was fifty-three. On his tomb, which poor
people in Concórdia still visit, we wrote: "From his lips we
heard, and from his life we learned: One who does not live
to serve does not deserve to live." From him I inherited
that internal flame, without which intellectual work turns
insipid; the option for the poor, without which our faith is
ineffective; and the unquenchable hunger for justice, without which we cease to be human. (Res Publica, October
1990)

I recall the day: May 9, 1949. Until that day I had never
thought of being a priest. There was a healthy tradition of
anticlericalism in my family, a precious heritage that we all
still cherish to this day. That particular day I saw a priest.
He was from Rio de Janeiro and he was giving us a talk on
vocations to the priesthood. He spoke of St. Francis and
St. Anthony, of the grandeur of being another Christ on
earth. He wound up with this: "Those who want to be
priests, raise your hands!" I heard every word he said and
felt an incredible glow of heat that rushed to my face. The
brief moment between his proposal and my response seemed
like an eternity. Someone inside me raised my hand. My
name was taken down and my father was notified. At home,
later, I bemoaned my action. Why would I want to be a
priest? I wanted to be a truck driver. That seemed the
grandest job in the world: to control and drive those big
monsters over our old highways. But my word had been
given, my life defined. (SL)

I am now over forty. I feel the weight of a life seasoned
by reflection and by the pursuit of the Word that sheds light
on everything. Sometimes I feel old. I think theologians
quickly reach a venerable old age because it is their task to

deal with the must problematic aspects of human mystery. Yet insofar as they internalize God, they regain — not exactly their youth, but the cheerfulness and flavor of all things. That is why I beg God every day that I not become bitter, or be unsettled, and that I always believe that what ultimately counts and has a future is being open, pure, transparent, generous, sincere, and good. For me the most important thing said about Jesus in the New Testament is not so much that he is God, Son of God, and Messiah, but that he went through the world doing good, curing some and consoling others. How I would like to see that said about everyone, myself included. (*Letter to Bishop Pedro Paulo Koop of Lins, Brazil, October 1979*)

Taking a quick look back at these past twenty-five years, I can see that my life has taken a particular direction: my first enthusiasm was for the Franciscan order, and for the priesthood, and then for theology; from theology I went on to the church, and from the church to the people; from the people to the poor, from the poor to humankind; from humankind to the mystery of creation. As things opened up and my horizon broadened, I experienced growth in interior authenticity and genuine freedom. My opportunities to be more human and therefore to feel united to the fate of all humankind and everything created became deeper within me. Today it is clear to me that the priesthood, religious life, and theology have radical meaning only if they bring us more directly into contact with other human beings, the men and women who are our traveling companions. (FB)

I was a voracious reader of the classics, the Greek thinkers first and then the Christian classics (Plato — all his works — Aristotle, Augustine, Boethius, the medieval masters, and many of the moderns). I have always wanted to measure myself against the great and to learn from them, not so much what they said, but how they came to say what they said. I have realized that they are, and will remain, magnificent, because they took intellectual life as an utterly serious endeavor, as a calling for the sake of which everything else had to be sacrificed. Back then, I used to read well into the night; I consumed holidays catching up on my reading; and I shunned sports in order to devote myself to reading the classics. I never was one to read the commentators or to go along with second-generation followers. (FB)

I am a theologian because I have always liked intellectual activity; when I undertook theology, it became a challenge to me. How are we to think about the problems of our people, about hunger and underdevelopment? How are we to think of the church in this world, which is so negative, so cruel, so much a nonworld? Later I went to study in Germany, and theology was different. But those questions stayed with me, and when I came home to go back to work, I returned to them. (*Jesus* magazine [Italy], February 1985)

I came back to Brazil in February 1970. In August I went to preach a retreat to missionary priests and religious in the Amazon jungle, in Manaus. It turned out to be a decisive crisis for me. I presented my theology to them, a theology that had moved beyond a certain alienation, but was not yet truly committed. I could see that I was not reaching my audience. They were concerned about the dire poverty of settlements along the rivers, the remoteness of the jungle, the dangers and the need for new responses to problems that were utterly new. Right away I sensed that this was a serious challenge for theological thinking. On the third day of the retreat my crisis was so intense that I was physically unable to speak. We broke up into groups. I tried as best I could to pull the conclusions together with quasi-theological or quasi-spiritual observations. But what had taken place was the existential shock I needed to move ahead intellectually. My subsequent thinking is still an effort to tame that initial experience: How are we to be Christians in the midst of overwhelming poverty, in the loneliness of the Amazon, in the injustice of social relations? We must act in a revolutionary and liberating way in order to furnish ourselves with reasons for our faith and so we may justify that faith in its claim to represent God's plan in history. (FB)

Starting in the mid-1980s, I realized ever more that the real issue of theology is actually not the church, but the people, and indeed humankind itself. From the standpoint of grace and salvation history, it is not the church that stands at the center of God's endeavor, but humankind. The whole of humankind is potentially the people of God. It is through solidarity, and the ties of community that are forged within it, that this people really becomes the people of God. The major issue is then: How does the Roman Catholic Church collaborate so as to encourage within humankind the emergence of solidarity, participation, communion, and goodwill among all? How does the church itself live those things, showing by example that it does what it proclaims? It then becomes rather disappointing to realize that while the church proclaims a marvelous utopia, it is others who try to bring it about. The church is a victim of its own feudal, discriminatory, and authoritarian style of organization. What makes it all worse is that the church has even made dogma out of this experiment in history, as though it were established by God and therefore inherently unquestionable. Such a conviction reminds us of absolute kings, who in order to dismiss the criticisms of the Enlightenment claimed to be of divine origin and therefore unassailable. (FB)

Prompted by the worldwide ecological crisis, during the last three years, I have been devoting my attention to the mystery of creation. In this respect the Franciscan theological and spiritual tradition is matchless. I have come to realize that the true and really radical mystery is the mystery of the world. It is a marvel that anything should exist. To know the *how* of the world is the task of science; to stand in awe at the fact of the world's existence is the ecstasy of

mysticism. So stated one of the most penetrating modern thinkers, Ludwig Wittgenstein.

We have created the myth that we are the center of the universe, that we are, as men and women, monarchs over the universe. On the basis of that title, we have taken over creation, we have overwhelmed the rhythms of nature, and we have assaulted all ecosystems. We have claimed that nature is ours. Today we realize that we also belong to nature. When we try to go deeper into the modern vision of what is created, by combining the general theory of relativity with quantum physics, we see to what extent matter—from subatomic particles to the most complex forms of living beings—is shot through with intentionality and spirituality. Everything is alive. The human being is a subsystem of the whole complex of creation, which is advancing through ever higher forms of consciousness and interiority. We are not the center of the universe. We live amid a vast living current that has gone forth from the bosom of the Trinity and is on its way back, encompassing the whole of creation. (FB)

How great a problem of conscience it would be for me if the people in their need were to beg me, "Father, stay with us because there is no one to care for us and for our faith!" That has happened to me two or three times already. Each time I was perplexed and very much disturbed deep down. I came to a very clear realization that these people do not need our theology; that is the luxury of an educated church. The people need someone to go along with them and encourage them in their faith. Could I refuse? On what grounds? What would happen if I encountered that question very bluntly and seriously? It would be a despicable and selfish pursuit of my own life not to respond to this new Macedonian we encounter in the Acts of the Apostles, the one whom Paul sees, pleading, "Come over to Macedonia and help us!" (Acts 16:9). (TEP)

Nothing I have ever written has been to convince others or to edify them, except what I wrote in my own defense vis-à-vis the former Holy Office. I have produced my theology in order to put down in writing my own reflections as a thinking Christian. The audience has always been myself. (FB)

I have suffered a great deal. We are used to the codified discourse of theology with its technical expressions. How are we to speak to people who are semiliterate? Without any theoretical assumptions except one's own life experience itself? It has to be as simple as possible. And how hard it is to be simple! There's no point in saying in theology or ethics, "on this issue there are five positions." The people are only interested in one, since they are not concerned with knowing but with living. And living means taking a stance, taking a position on issues. Therefore only one position is worthwhile, the one on which we make our decision.

I have recognized that in contact with the people theology loses its irresponsible dilettantism. Everything has its weight. The people take every word seriously because those words have consequences in their lives. I have never felt so pressured as in these weekly sessions with the people. You discover that you are out of contact with your cultural roots; our language is class-based, and can be understood only by those who have gone to school and even to the university. What is worse, we think the way we speak is absolute, scientific, and universally valid. You need only be confronted by the people for an hour to realize that the language of theology is quite particular, that of a privileged group in church and society. All of a sudden I felt that my whole theology, in the way it was expressed, was worthless. It is like going to the United States bulging with millions of cruzeiros, and wanting to buy something with them. You may have millions, but there they are worthless. (TEP)

My period of silence was very hard* since the theologian deals with the word and we Latin Americans speak more than we write, although I had already done a bit of writing. Our theology is worked out in groups, as we work with communities, homilies, and contacts with bishops. The word is our weapon; yet suddenly I found that my tool had been taken away, and so obviously I suffered a great deal.

I was a victim of this unacceptable method, the very method used by the military in Brazil, and which the church in Brazil had criticized for many years. Suddenly Rome was doing the same thing as the military. I regarded it as unacceptable, but I took it in a spirit of communion with the many thousands of persons silenced on this continent, with the silenced cultures, the cultures of silence of the native peoples and the blacks. They are never allowed to speak, and when they do speak, almost nobody pays attention. I actually felt to some extent in communion with all this, and even privileged, since many have suffered a great deal more than I. (*La Jornada* [Mexico], December 1986)

During the year of silence to which I was subjected, I matured a great deal. I stopped being theologically naive when I came to realize that, in the church's internal con-

---

*As a result of questions raised by Cardinal Joseph Ratzinger, Prefect of the Congregation for the Doctrine of the Faith, regarding his book *Church: Charism and Power*, Boff was ordered in 1985 to maintain a penitential silence. The order was lifted eleven months later.
—EDITOR.

flicts, it is not only religious concerns that weigh most heavily, but also other hidden, non-gospel, objectives.

Before my punishment, I thought that theological thinking of a liberationist tendency was rising in the church. I did not realize clearly enough that there was another drive for ascendancy in the church, one of a conservative character. In my suffering I have learned to be more realistic and more concrete, and I have a better understanding of the weight of various tendencies in the church. (*Fôlha de São Paulo* [Brazil], May 1986)

Some silences are golden, just as others are leaden. In this case I think silence had a great impact, since the support I received on various levels, especially at the grassroots, with an average of a hundred letters a day, seems to have left a big impression on the Vatican, and on the pope himself, who was not aware that this theology was connected to a journey by society itself, by the oppressed as a whole. (*Gazeta do Acre*, January 1987)

The purpose of the silencing was to enable me to have time to think and ponder more deeply my responsibilities as a theologian. That was what I did. I realized that the issues confronting liberation theologians are relevant not only to our Latin American church but also to the fate of the universal church. (*O Globo*, April 1986)

I don't think I am a heretic—leaving aside the fact that many heretics have later been made saints. The important thing is not whether Rome or I will be the winner. The important thing is the truth that makes us free. I believe in the church that stands alongside the poor. We liberation theologians believe that the truth of the church of the poor is deeply rooted in the gospel, and Rome has to understand that. In Rome I feel the power of the institution more than the power of truth. (*Der Spiegel* [Germany], September 1984)

Personally I am calm and always have been. I acknowledge the function of the church's teaching authority, but also that of theology. The theologian's role is to delve more deeply, to open up new paths, and to try to provide an ultimate meaning to human existence, which is brimming with conflicts of all kinds. . . .

Unlike many others, I do not think it necessary to be set up in an academic chair in order to do theology; it may be that today the "chair" of the people and of life offer more scope than the professorial chair, since that is where the major problems and the demanding challenges are to be found. That is where the suffering is. Even more than wonder, it is suffering that triggers thought. That much, at least, the poor have taught us. (*O Globo*, December 1980)

So far I have never lost a minute of sleep over my problems with the Vatican. I really don't think that these problems are worth losing sleep over. The things they condemn in my theology I also condemn. They are attributing to me things I do not hold. The issue is not really Boff as a liberation theologian; they are attacking a movement that jeopardizes the power existing in the church, and I represent that movement. (*La Vanguardia* [Spain], September 1990)

Currently my relations with the Vatican are like those of any other Christian — that is, none, officially. I continue my work, I do my theology. They have a problem with me; I have never had a problem with Rome. I suffer continual interference and surveillance, but I try to maintain a Franciscan spirit, with a degree of good humor, aware that the major issues for theology and the church today are unrelated to these petty controversies the Vatican stirs up against me. That is why I do not pay much attention to them. I am just penalized because it takes up my time and occasionally my tranquility, when I have to explain and make myself understood to those authorities. (*Fôlha de São Paulo*, October 1990)

What enkindles prophetic wrath within me is that there is no room for criticism in the church, as even society itself allows today. The press is a critical force, and if it provides adequate information, that information will itself pronounce judgment. What the church lacks are mechanisms for circulating information that might allow for a critique of the way it is institutionalized—for its own benefit. The church is still very feudal, very authoritarian, we might say. (*Diário de Pernambuco*, December 1978)

My greatest commitment is to the poor. I continue in the church because I have faith in the gospel and in the church as the space where I live and struggle, and because the church is neither the pope, nor the Roman curia, nor even the Holy Office. The church represents the poor families who live with me and those who believe in the gospel. (*Tribuna de Petrópolis*, November 1990)

It is more important to be a Christian than a theologian. Even if I were kicked out, I would never abandon the church of the poor.

I would not regard being kicked out as a personal sort of drama. I might even see it as something that could serve to push me much more deeply into grassroots work.

I do not see such a possibility as a failure, a break in my life, or loss of direction. (*IstoÉ*, June 1983)

I will remain a Catholic, even if they cancel my ticket. (*O Globo*, December 1979)

The longer I live, the more my perception of mystery grows. Mystery is much more than an enigma. As the ancients knew better than we, mystery has an ultimate meaning beyond our grasp, but which passes through us, uses us as a subsystem of something greater, and proceeds on its way until it rests in the very heart of God. Each of us is playing a role, as in a theater. We choose neither the work nor our role; we do not know how it will actually end. At most we see that we are at the service of the One who claims to be alpha and omega, beginning and end — in short, the Lord of life and history. (FB)

I feel like a mere servant who has simply done what he had to do. And there is still much to be done. May it please God that the time be propitious for us to grow toward God, toward others, and toward our own heart. In the symphony of life it has perhaps been my lot to play percussion, those instruments that make a lot of noise. But truth is symphonic. When everything is put together, even notes that are off key merge into the music. In this global symphony where we all play under God's direction, I am quite content. I pay more attention to the whole than to the parts, and more to the conductor than to myself. I myself will be symphonic insofar as I listen to and love all the other instruments and sounds. May that be God's will and may God grant me the strength. (FB)

Living in Accord
with the Spirit

We do not experience the spirit as a part of the human being, but as a living whole. Spirit denotes the energy and vitality of all human manifestations. In this sense spirit is not opposed to the body but rather includes it. Spirit is opposed to death. Hence the great opposition is not between spirit and matter, or between body and soul, but between death and life. (*Vozes*, September-October 1990)

Self-realization is not the work of reason, which discourses from one point to another, but of the recollection of spirit gathering the wealth present in each situation. Spirit is not something alongside the body nor is it the highest form of reason. Spirit is the way of being of those humans who can discover the meaning of each thing. Hence it is character-istic of the spirit to attain the wisdom of life — that is, to live the mystery of God deciphered in each situation. It is the ability to be whole in everything we do. That is what is proper to the Spirit. Spirituality means being able to live in this manner, God in all things. Spirituality is not a science or a technique, but a way of living. (VSE)

The human being is a composite of body and soul. This does not mean that in the human there are two things, body plus soul, which united give rise to the human being. Body is the entire human (body + soul) insofar as he or she is limited, held to the restrictions of the earthly situation. Soul is the entire human as oriented toward the Infinite, insofar as he or she is an entity insatiably striving toward complete fulfillment. The concrete human being is the difficult and tense unity of these two poles. ... The body is how the spirit lives in the world, incarnate in matter. (VAM)

Rooted in the world (flesh), human beings are nevertheless not lost in the world. They are the only beings in creation who can transcend the limits in which they live. Recalling the past, and stretching out in hope toward the future, they can answer the appeals of the present. An infinite desire lies within them, and so their thoughts dwell in the stars and the heavens. They can identify and establish a covenant with God. Having experienced God as Absolute, they relativize the historical, religious, political, and ideological powers that seek to present themselves as ultimate. On the basis of the absolute they can glimpse, human beings laugh good naturedly when the human theater becomes too serious. (VSE)

Every spiritual experience means an encounter with a new and challenging face of God growing out of the great challenges of ongoing history. Major sociological changes bear within themselves an ultimate meaning, a supreme exigency that religious spirits detect as deriving from God's mystery. God has meaning only when actually emerging as what is radically important in a given situation, in both its shadows and its lights. Thus God comes to be seen not simply as a category defined in religious terms, but as the occurrence of meaning, hope, and absolute future for human beings and their history. Human beings thereby experience the very mystery of God. (VSE)

What do we live for? To love and relate as family with others who have become our neighbors, our brothers or sisters. Such a way of living means overcoming all hatred, selfish instinct, and vindictiveness, which are embodiments of a life direction in accordance with the flesh. Living in accordance with the spirit includes being completely reconciled, even with our enemy. One whose starting point for living is God begins to act like God, who "loves the ungrateful and wicked" (Lk 6:35), and "provides sun and rain for the just and the unjust" (Mt 5:45). (VSE)

The postulate of history and of the Christian faith is one of seeking a complete liberation, one that embraces every dimension of human life: physical and spiritual, personal and collective, historical and transcendent. No reductionism, whether it be spiritual or material in orientation, will do justice to the unity of humankind, to the unique design of the Creator, and to the central reality of Jesus' proclamation of the kingdom of God, which embraces creation as a whole. (LP)

Those who think mystics are withdrawn from the world are mistaken. It is they who are most committed. (*O Globo*, December 1979)

Religious life is a specific way of being in the world: it is a matter of seeing everything and living everything as shot through with God's presence. If God is the only absolute, then everything that exists is a revelation of God. Seeking God's will, detecting God's presence, and deciphering the meaning of God's activity (signs of the times) in all that happens: such is the anguish and task of every truly religious soul. (VSE)

In biblical terms, the Spirit is like a tornado or a whirlwind. It is a transforming force like the love that is stronger than death. The Spirit is not something ethereal and vague, as it is imagined in our culture. Wouldn't our spirituality be dynamic if we were to accept the Spirit as vital and ever innovating energy? (STMC)

The Spirit has been poured forth over all. It dwells in people's hearts, giving them enthusiasm, courage, and determination. It consoles the afflicted, keeps utopia alive in human minds and in the imagination of society — the utopia of a humankind completely redeemed — and provides the power to anticipate that utopia, even through revolutions within history. The Spirit is a divine person, alongside the Son and the Father, who emerges simultaneously with them, and is united to them through love, communion, and the divine life itself. (STMC)

Nature is not mute; the rocks speak, the sea expresses itself, and the firmament sings God's glory. Nothing is just tossed in and left to chance. Everything is related and enters into communion: the wind with the rock, the rock with the land, the land with the sun, and the sun with the universe. Everything is in perichoresis, bathed in the communion of the Blessed Trinity. (STMC)

The cross of life is heavier the more it is borne in solitude. And we need so little to relieve it! All we need is for someone to approach and stand by our side. A few words, something whispered, a pat on the shoulder are enough. Sometimes just sitting together and sharing a cup serves to mend the torn fabric of our life. (VSR)

Every existing being bears the mark of the Father, and hence always presents itself as a mystery; bears the mark of the Son, and hence can be comprehended as a brother and sister; bears the mark of the Holy Spirit, and hence can nourish our spiritual dimension. (STMC)

Christ's first word is not cross, nor is his final word death. The first is joy, and the last is life. (VSR)

To imitate Christ does not mean to copy or even imitate his gestures. It means having the same attitude and the same spirit as Jesus, incarnating it in our concrete situation, which is different from that of Jesus. To imitate is "to have the same sentiments as Christ" (Phil 2:5); to be, like him, un-selfish; to feel with others and identify with them: to per-severe until the end in love, in faith, in goodness of the human heart. It is not to fear being critical, challenging a religious or social situation that does not humanize human beings or make them free for others and for God. It is to have the courage to be generous and at the same time main-tain good sense; to use creative imagination; to be faithful to the laws that foster an atmosphere of love and human comprehension. (JCL)

Everything is Christ's. He did not just introduce some-thing new—that is, himself and his resurrection. He also came to reveal the holiness of all things. All things—yesterday, today, and always—are filled with him. What is specifically Christian is the capacity to see his activity and efficacy in all the articulations of human history, especially those where humanity most reveals itself as human. Christian sacramentalism is Christian because it knows enough to relate the "natural" sacraments to the mystery of Christ. Everything that is true, holy, and good is already Christian, even when the label "Christian" is not used. Nothing is rejected. Everything is taken over. Everything is read and interpreted in the light of the history of Christ's mystery. And so we get transfiguration: in its own specific and different way, each and every thing becomes a Christian sacrament. It comes from Christ and leads to Christ. (SL)

The Christian tradition is familiar with the ascetic saint, who tames his or her passions and faithfully observes the laws of God and the church. It is almost unaware of political saints and activist saints. In the liberation process there has emerged a situation propitious for another kind of holiness: besides struggling against one's own passions (a perennial task), one struggles against the mechanisms of exploitation that destroy community. (VSE)

Holding to the Christ of the poor means being a "contemplative in liberation": *contemplativus in liberatione*. It implies a new way of seeking holiness and mystical union with God. A spiritual collision with God's new manifestation has produced specific new traits in the spirituality lived and practiced by so many Christians committed to the integral liberation of their sisters and brothers. This spiritual collision is the basis of the theology of liberation. (FE)

With the assurance of resurrection, cheerfulness has come into the world. Being cheerful means being able to celebrate, within the ambiguity of the present situation—retreat and advance, violence and peacemaking—the triumph of life over death, the victory of affirmation over negation. (VAM)

I heard an aged confrere, wise and good, perfect and holy, say:

If you feel the call of the Spirit, then be holy with all your soul, with all your heart, and with all your strength.

If, however, because of human weakness you cannot be holy, then be perfect with all your soul, with all your heart, and with all your strength.

But if you cannot be perfect because of vanity in your life, then be good with all your soul, with all your heart, and with all your strength.

Yet, if you cannot be good because of the trickery of the Evil One, then be wise with all your soul, with all your heart, and with all your strength.

If, in the end, you can be neither holy, nor perfect, nor good, nor wise because of the weight of your sins, then carry this weight before God and surrender your life to the divine mercy.

If you do this, without bitterness, with all humility, and with a joyous spirit due to the tenderness of a God who loves the sinful and ungrateful, then you will begin to feel what it is to be wise, you will learn what it is to be good, you will slowly aspire to be perfect, and finally you will long to be holy.

If you do all this, with all your soul, with all your heart, and with all your strength, then I assure you, my brother, you will be on the path of Saint Francis, you will not be far from the kingdom of God. (SF)

Mystery of Life

When we entrust ourselves to the mystery of life; when we stop belonging to ourselves alone; when we stop putting ourselves first and give ourselves in loving service to others; when we believe and hope that nothing escapes the design of the ultimate mystery, that no evil or dis-grace can separate us from the love of God—when we do these things, then we experience the reality that Christianity calls grace. (LG)

Grace steeps human history and permeates the human heart. So does sin. Concretely, human history is arrayed in a difficult dialectic of sin and grace, obedience and rebellion—the realization and the frustration of God's plan in history existing side by side. (WTLP)

Grace is not something from God; it is God, God's self-communication, given as meaning, hope, love, courage. (LG)

Heaven is not only absolute human realization nor merely the vision, enjoyment, and possession of God by human beings but also, and principally, the possession of human beings by God. God will become flesh in each of us. God will assume, in the degree proper to each of us, the human nature of every human being. God will render himself concrete — eschatologically, in heaven — in the fulfillment of that possibility to whose realization we have all been called. This is our supreme vocation: that we should be called and be able to renounce ourselves altogether in order to be entirely God's. (FE)

Grace and salvation are a joint endeavor of persons and their worlds, of persons and the communities with which they share life. Each is responsible for the other's grace. Each should be a sacrament of salvation for the other. Herein lies the deepest meaning of love for neighbor, which is to embrace even our enemy. Grace and salvation entail universal solidarity. The concrete course of divine love passes through human love for everyone whom we approach. This is the privileged way God chose to reveal who God is: a mystery of love in self-communication, causing other loves to exist, and enabling them to love even as God loves. The grace of God becomes history in the history of love at work in the world. (LG)

The sacred is not to be found primarily in objects held to be such. The sacred is that dimension of depth that confers wholeness and unity on the inner life. In our culture, which is thoroughly imbued with the Judeo-Christian experience — in other cultures there would be other reference points such as Buddha, Atman, and so forth — we refer to this as *imago Dei*, the image of God glowing at the center of our inner life. (*Vozes*, September-October 1990)

God did not become incarnate in Jesus of Nazareth simply to divinize human beings, but also to humanize them and make them more humane, freeing them from the load of inhumanity they bear as a result of their past history. (TCL)

Through the Spirit the feminine has attained ultimate fulfillment. Truly and intimately acting in Mary, the Spirit made her to be mother of God. Since she was united to the Holy Spirit, what was born of her was Holy, the Son of God (Lk 1:35). The feminine in Mary thus becomes part of God's own mystery. As the masculine in Jesus is divinized by the Son, so the feminine in Mary is divinized by the Holy Spirit. That is why the mariological principle is not something marginal in the history of God's revelation; it rounds out the christological principle. Together they reveal the mysterious face of the Father and elevate human beings — who are always both masculine and feminine in varying proportions — toward their final destiny in God. (AM)

Jesus' liberation assumes a twofold aspect. On the one hand, Jesus proclaims a total liberation of all history and not merely of one segment of that history; on the other, he anticipates this totality in a concrete process of partial liberations ever open to this totality. Had Jesus proclaimed a utopia of blessed outcome for the world deprived of any anticipation in history, he would have been fostering human phantasmagorias deprived of all credibility. Had he introduced partial liberation without the perspective of totality and the future, he would have been frustrating the hopes he himself had awakened, and he would have fallen into a self-contradictory immediatism of the Reign. But both dimensions of the Reign of God, the "already" and the "not yet," are found in Jesus' activity and are found there in dialectical tension. (FE)

The future of the world is that it will be able to reveal God in a perfect and utterly clear fashion. (VAM)

Deciding for one's own fulfillment entails deciding for the new order of the world and how it is to be changed. Human beings can never attain fulfillment without the world, but only within it, for the world is actually the human being extended and incarnate in matter. (TCL)

Silence with regard to God may be a sign both of deep religion and of what is true about secularization. In Simone Weil's wonderful observation, "To determine whether someone is truly religious we should not observe how they speak of God, but how they speak of the world." (VSE)

History is pregnant with Christ, and "the whole of creation is groaning and suffering the pains of childbirth," awaiting the birth to come. (VAM)

Death stands as the most utterly privileged situation in life, the one in which the human breaks through to complete spiritual maturation, where intelligence, will, sensitivity, and freedom can be exercised with complete spontaneity for the first time, freed of the external conditioning factors and the limitations inherent in our situation-in-the-world. Only at this point does there appear, also for the first time, the possibility of a completely free decision expressing the entire human being vis-à-vis God, others, and the cosmos. (VAM)

Hope translates the openness of human beings to tomorrow, where they hope to find some meaning that will fulfill the life they are living today. Hope is not just the future as future. It is the future as *already* present, tasted, and experienced but *not yet* received and fully realized. Hence it is also future . . . The principle of hope is not exhausted in the future that human beings can plan and construct. It goes beyond all human constructions in history. It ever remains metaphysically unsatisfied because it always feels called to better things. Only the absolute future, the realization of utopia, can quiet the heart steeped in hope. God is thus seen as utopia, as the absolute and total concretization of all that can be . . .

Living in grace, human beings live grounded in the absolute future, God. They encounter God in their concrete hopes for a more human life, for better housing, and for a more just and fraternal society . . . By virtue of this absolute hope, Christians do two things. On the one hand, they involve themselves in the work of concretizing human hopes because they see their relation to the absolute hope. On the other hand, they see these concretizations as relative because they are not absolutely identical with the Absolute that is to come. (LG)

Hell is an absurd existence petrified in the absurd. (VAM)

Grace signifies the presence of God in the world and in human beings. When God chooses to be present, the sick are made well, the fallen are raised up, the sinners are made just, the dead come back to life, the oppressed experience freedom, and the despairing feel consolation and warm intimacy.

Grace also signifies the openness of human beings to God. It is the ability of human beings to relate to the Infinite, to enter upon a dialogue that wins them their humanity day by day and rewards them with deification.

Grace is always an encounter between a God who gives himself and a human being who does likewise. By its very nature grace is the breaking down of realms or worlds that are closed in upon themselves. Grace is relationship, exodus, communion, encounter, openness, and dialogue. It is the history of two freedoms, the meeting of two loves.

For this reason, grace signifies the reconciliation of heaven and earth, of God and humans, of time and eternity . . . Grace is oneness and reconciliation; hence it is synonymous with salvation, with perfect identity between humans and God. (LG)

Heaven means being completely able to see, not the surface of things, but their heart. Heaven is so much a feast for the eyes that the vision of our earthly eyes is as through a dark mirror (cf. 1 Cor 13:12) in comparison with what is seen in heaven. This is what we mean when we say: heaven is the convergence of all the potentialities and energies of the world and humankind. It is homeland and hearth of our identity, where all things find themselves in their ultimate depth and fulfillment.

Heaven should not be set in opposition to this world. It should be seen as the fullness of this world, now free of everything that limits or injures, divides or binds it. (VAM)

As understood in Christianity, resurrection does not mean the revivification of a corpse but the utter fulfillment of the potential of the human being, body and soul. (VAM)

What is resurrected is our personal self, that which we have created internally during our earthly life, the self that has always entailed a relationship with the world and hence our body. We may even say that in the resurrection all will attain the body they deserve, one that corresponds to their self and expresses it completely and appropriately. (RCNR)

Love: Leaven of Resurrection

Love means letting God happen in our life. To allow God to happen in our life means being divinized and letting God be humanized. (LG)

To make love one's norm of life and moral conduct is to impose something very difficult on oneself. It is easier to live within laws and prescriptions that foresee and determine everything. It is difficult to create a norm inspired by love for each moment. Love knows no limits. It calls for creative imagination. It exists only in giving oneself to, and putting oneself at the service of, others. And it is only in giving that one has. This is the "law" of Christ: that we love one another as God has loved us. (JCL)

Perfect love is not a love that loves everyone and everything on account of God (*propter Deum*) or in God (*in Deo*). Perfect love is a love that loves everyone and everything because it discovers the lovableness of all as the concrete presence of God's own love. (LG)

Forgiveness is love in pain. A trusting self-abandon is the total decentering of ourselves and our total recentering on Someone who infinitely transcends us. Forgiveness and self-surrender mean risking Mystery, throwing in our lot with that ultimate vessel of Meaning in which we participate more than we dream. This is the opportunity offered to human freedom. Men and women can take advantage of the offer, and rest secure. Or they can let it slip by, and founder in despair. Forgiveness and trust are our tools for not letting hopelessness have the last word. They constitute the supreme deed of human grandeur.

How do we know that this trust, this de-centering, achieves ultimate Meaning? By the resurrection. Resurrection is the fullness and manifestation of the Life that resonates within life and within death. The only way for the Christian to make this assertion is to look at the crucified Jesus — who now lives. (PCPW)

Whenever in our moral life goodness triumphs over the instincts of hatred, whenever one heart opens to another heart, whenever a just attitude is built up and space is created for God, there the resurrection is gaining a foothold. Death merely frees the seeds so that the luxuriant flowering of life may explode and implode. (WTLP)

Grace and love come down to the same thing. Human beings need love, but it must be free, gratuitous love. Only such love can bring fulfillment, joy, and indescribable happiness. Only those who know true love can comprehend the most sacred words of Christianity: that God is love (1 Jn 4:8–16), that love comes from God (1 Jn 4:7), and that love will never cease to exist (1 Cor 13:8). It is the grace of God in the grace of human beings. (LG)

Love, as understood in the New Testament, means the ability to transform servant-master relationships into those of brothers and sisters. Christ proposed not sacred power (*hierarquia*) but sacred service (*hierodulia*). (DHM)

According to the gospel, one's neighbor is not the person next door, one's fellow citizen, or one's brother or sister in the faith. My neighbor is every human being from the moment I approach him or her with love. (TCL)

Among human beings true power is based on love. The power of love does not lie in controlling others but in serving them, not in enslaving them, but in respecting their freedom. Where freedom does not reign, there cannot be love. (DHM)

Human life unfolds in a very complex web of relationships. Its purpose and identity are to be found in the capacity to be-in-others. It is through what is different from themselves that human beings come to themselves. Insofar as they are able to assimilate and receive what is different and outside them, they commune and create community. Living humanly is always living-with. (VSE)

Love is either gratuitous or it is not love. That is why grace is defined as the communication of God's love to human beings. (LG)

If Christ frees human beings from laws, he does not hand them over to living with abandon or to irresponsibility. Rather, he creates ties and bonds that are stronger than those of the law. Love ought to bind all human beings together. (JCL)

If individuals receive communion, they ought to be elements of communion in the group in which they live. If they celebrate the sacrifice of Christ and his violent death, they should be ready to undergo the same sacrifice and to live their Christian faith in the same manner. This includes persecution, arrest, and violent death as normal things. If they administer or receive baptism, they should be witnesses to the faith in their community. If they seek reconciliation and find pardon in the sacrament of penance, they should be signs of reconciliation amid the conflicts of society. (SL)

Without conversion, the celebration of a sacrament is an offense against God. It means casting pearls before swine, choosing to perform the acts embodying Christ's maximum visibility in the world without adequate interior purification. One must have one's heart in one's hand for encounter, be pure for love, and be reconciled for feasting. (SL)

What we have is simply a shift of focus. One church thinks of God, prayer, Mass, the sacraments. The other is focused more on love for neighbor. It is a matter of practicing justice rather than talking about justice. More than preaching the reign of God it seeks to bring about God's reign. One church does not rule out the other. Ultimately, however, we are going to be judged more by love than by the number of times we went to Mass or by our faith in dogmas like the Immaculate Conception or papal infallibility. (IstoÉ, June 1983)

The monastery doorbell rang at 11:30 A.M. An old woman was at the door, clutching a lantern, and all wrapped up in a gray cloak. She was carrying a small package, and said "It's for the young foreign priest who was at midnight Mass." They sent for me. With few words she handed me the package, "You are a long way from your country. Far from your loved ones. Here is a small present for you. Today is Christmas for you too." She pressed it firmly into my hand and disappeared into the night under the blessing of the snow.

Alone in my room while recalling images of Christmas at home, a lot like this but without the snow, I reverently opened the package. It was a big candle. Deep red. All carved. With a hefty metal base. A light brightened the lonely night. Flickering long shadows were cast against the wall. I no longer felt alone. Far away from my country the whole Christmas miracle had taken place: the celebration of the fellowship of all human beings. Someone had understood the Child's message: make the stranger a neighbor and the foreigner kinfolk. (SL)

Theology as Scholarship and as Life

Theology is faith seeking understanding. Understanding means judging, criticizing, and knowing how to make distinctions. Hence theology is a kind of faith that is reflective and critical. There is no such thing as theology without faith, because we cannot speak of God the way we speak of objects. Either we are speaking under the impact of the divine reality or we are simply dealing with the history of religious ideas, something that an atheist can also do quite competently. Hence in theology we cannot speak of God as though God could stand on some higher ground from which we might be able to glimpse God; we can, however, speak of God and from God insofar as we speak of human life as affected by God's divine and unfathomable reality. (VSE)

I think every human person is a theologian. Each person raises ultimate questions: where do I come from, where am I going, what does suffering mean, what is the ultimate destiny of the world, what can be hoped for beyond this world, what meaning is there to the suffering of so many who are innocent? When we think about all this and pursue these questions all the way, we are doing theology. And if at the end of this pondering we find that everything has meaning, despite all the absurdities, then we are dropping anchor in that reality that religions call God. God only has meaning when connected to such ultimate questions and in response to them. Professional theologians like myself specialize in these issues. We create a specialized discourse. We connect this reflection on God, and based on God, with all things human. Our basic concern is to discern the signs of God's presence in the world, in social processes, in the struggles of the oppressed, in the tender affection of those who love one another, in the deeds of solidarity by all who choose to strive for a better society for those now outcast, in the sensitivity of conscience, and in the depths of our own hearts. (*Res Publica*, October 1989)

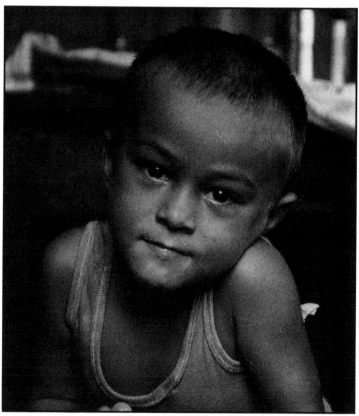

It is important to distinguish what is faith and what is
explication of faith. So, to say that God is Father, Son, and
Holy Spirit is an expression of faith; to say that God is one
nature and three persons is an explication of faith. We
welcome faith with open hearts; explications of faith can
be debated and even rejected. Faith is response to divine
revelation; explications of faith are the responses of reason
to the questions raised by faith. (TS)

Theology must return to the faith from which it arises —
not to eliminate faith or add confusion, but to nourish it,
and make it clearer. Certainly theology is a speculative science. It is not enough to be pious and good; you have to
be intelligent and insightful. But speculation is only one
aspect of theology. Ultimately it aims at being a practical
science. It should end in a practice of love and joy. Simply
believing in one God — even the devils believe in that (as
St. James assures us [2:19]), and their theology is obviously
sharper than that of the best theologian. But they do not
have love, and thus "they are nothing" (1 Cor 15:2). To
see in order to do; to know in order to love: such is the
ultimate function of theology. (FE)

The purpose of theology is to present the essence of faith
in such a way that it can be existentially lived by the faithful
as well as being plausible to human reason in each age. The
rule of faith must preserve the essence of faith but without
maintaining it in immutable formulas. What is extraordinary
about the Christian faith is that it always maintains its identity throughout its various historical changes and distinct
formulations. This was the case with the gospels and will
continue throughout history. As our experience of the world
changes so do our problems and questions. If theology does
not consider these historical factors and does not include

them in its presentation of Christian faith, then the rule of faith becomes a caricature of empty, fictional realities. (CCP)

The criterion of true theology is not whether other theologians approve, but whether it produces faith, hope, and charity. And today we add, if it brings about change in society, justice, and fellowship. If it does that, then it is true, and it is theology. If another theology, regardless of its theoretical sophistication, fails to do that, it may also be theology—but it is the devil's theology. (*Fôlha de São Paulo*, July 1983)

Philosophers like to talk about God as the absolute. There is something wrong about such terminology: it always sets up a fundamental dualism between the absolute and the relative, eternity and time, God and the world. We Christians prefer to speak of the communion of the divine persons which is always inclusive, since it also encompasses humankind, the world, and time. (STMC)

Theologians do not live in the clouds. They are social actors with a particular place in society. They produce knowledge, data, and meanings by using instruments that the situation offers and allows them. Their findings are also addressed to a particular audience. Thus theologians stand within an overall social context. The themes and emphases of a given christology flow from what seems relevant to the theologian on the basis of his or her social standpoint. In that sense we must maintain that no christology is or can be neutral. Every christology is partisan and committed. (JCL)

For centuries theology was argumentative. It sought to speak to the minds of human beings and convince them of the truth of religion. Its success was meager. Usually it was convincing only to those already convinced. Theology elaborated its themes under the illusion that God, the divine plan of salvation, the future promised to humanity, and the mystery of Jesus Christ as God and human being could be accepted intellectually before people had accepted them in their real lives and undergone a transformation of heart. Forgotten, at least in the manuals of theology and apologetics, was the fact that religious truth is never an abstract formula or the end-product of logical reasoning. It is basically and primarily a vital experience, an encounter with ultimate meaning. Only then comes the cultural articulation and linkup, which translates it into formulas and explicitates its inherent rational element. (SL)

An encounter with the divine Mystery lies at the root of all religious doctrine. This encounter evokes a deep experience embracing all our humanity: emotions, reason, will, desire, and heart. The first reaction, and expression of pleasure, is praise, worship, and proclamation. After that comes the task of appropriating and translating this experience-encounter, the task of devout reasoning. This is the state at which doctrines and creeds come into being. (TS)

Conscience is God within us. Seneca was right when he wrote, "Conscience is God within you, alongside you, and with you." All human beings realize that their conscience is greater than they are. They do not have power over it. They did not create it; nor can they destroy it. But they can disobey it. Deny it. Violate it. But hush it up, that they cannot do. (DHM)

Christic Structure and Christian Faith

God's proposal emerges within the human conscience, the place where God speaks to each person. Whenever conscience feels responsible and experiences a challenge to go outside of itself, to accept the other, to assume the task, there God is making a proposal. The proposal may emerge within life, in the signs of the times, in the exigencies of the concrete situation. Whenever we are called to grow, love, get outside ourselves, open ourselves to others and God, to assume responsibility before our conscience and others, there we have a proposal that demands a faithful response. If we open up and love, we have the concretization of a christic structure. (JCL)

The salvation proclaimed by Christianity is all-embracing. It is not restricted to economic, political, social, and ideological emancipation, but neither can it be realized without them. (JCL)

To have faith, biblically, means more than holding to certain truths; it also implies a serene trust in a mysterious, ultimate sense of reality. We can say to the world, to life, to everything that exists: amen, so be it! This is why the opposite of faith is fear and the inability to entrust oneself confidently to a greater power. (LP)

Faith has always tried to discern the meaning of the phrase: Jesus is true God and true man. Faith that tries to understand is called theology — in this case, christology. Theology does not seek, nor should it, to control faith. On the contrary, it seeks to help and clarify faith. It seeks to be one among the possible forms of faith: critical, rational, scientific (if possible), always searching for a better analysis of the life of faith. It does this not to violate its intimacy but to detect the rationality and gracious logic of God, and thus to love God in a more intense and human way. To speak in a christological manner can never mean to speak *about* Jesus. (JCL)

The senses do not sense, the eyes cannot capture the heart of things. Faith opens up an illuminating access to the ultimate innerness of the world, where it reveals itself as the temple of God and of the transfigured cosmic Christ. The Lord is not far from us. The material elements are sacraments that put us in communion with him, because they, in the most intimate part of their being, pertain to the very reality of Christ. (JCL)

In their most pristine and positive form, religions are the institutional forms that translate humanity's relationship to the Absolute. Religion is always a reaction to a prior action. It is the human response to God's proposal. It is an original phenomenon that cannot be reduced to something more basic. It bears witness to humanity's openness to some transcendent reality, to something of definitive importance, to a transcendent meaning that transfigures reality with all its contradictions.

This theological valuation of religion does not mean that everything in that religion is legitimate. It can contain diabolic elements that do a bad job of translating the demands

of God and the mystery of humanity into words, deeds, and
ethical requirements. Yet despite all the ambiguities of the
world's religions (including the religion of the Bible and
Christianity), they are vehicles that communicate grace, forgiveness, and the future that God promises to human beings.
(LG)

Christianity is concrete and consistent living in a christic
structure, a living of that which Jesus of Nazareth lived:
total openness to others and the Great Other, indiscrimi-
nate love, unshakable fidelity to the voice of conscience,
and the overcoming of whatever chains human beings to
their own egoism. (JCL)

Faith would not believe what it professes had it not been
revealed by God. In this respect reverent silence commu-
nicates more than the jabbering of our words. (FE)

The Christian God is the eternal communion of the divine
three—Father, Son, and Holy Spirit. They are eternally
pouring forth toward one another, so much so that they
make up a single movement of love, communication, and
encounter. How are we to understand this reality better?
We are not unveiling the mystery of God here; rather we
seek to grasp the divine movement so as to be able to live
out better the presence and activity of the Blessed Trinity
in the world and in the course of our own life. Biblical
theology has come up with a word to express this divine
dynamic: life. God is understood as a life that is eternal,
one bestowing and protecting all life that is threatened, like
that of the poor and those who suffer injustice. Jesus himself, the incarnate Son, presented himself as one who came
to bring life, and life in abundance (Jn 10:10). (STMC)

Wherever we may be, God is Emmanuel, and is journeying alongside us. Although each of us is following his or her own path, deep bonds that can be comprehended only by faith unite us and make us God's people moving through history. (TEP)

The theme of Christ's preaching was neither himself nor the church but the kingdom of God. "Kingdom of God" signifies the realization of a utopia cherished in human hearts, total human and cosmic liberation. It is the new situation of an old world, now replete with God and reconciled with itself. In a word, it could be said that the kingdom of God means a total global, structural revolution of the old order, brought about by God and only by God. (JCL)

The kingdom, although not of this world in its origin — it comes from God — is nevertheless among us, manifesting itself in processes of liberation. Liberation is the act of gradually delivering reality from the various captivities to which it is historically subject and which run counter to God's historical project — which is the upbuilding of the kingdom, a kingdom in which everything is oriented to God, penetrated by God's presence, and glorified, on the cosmic level as on the personal level (the level of divinization). Liberations show forth the activity of eschatological salvation by anticipation, as the leaven of today in the dough of a reality fully to be transfigured in the eschaton. (SAL)

For those who see everything in terms of God, the entire world is one grand sacrament. Every thing and every historical event appear as sacraments of God and God's divine will. But that is only possible for those who see God as alive.

For those who do not, the world is opaque and merely immanent. Insofar as people allow themselves, by toil and effort, to be taken and penetrated by God, they are rewarded with the divine transparence of all things. (SL)

God's self-communication occurs in both the sacred and the profane. Both stand under God's loving activity and are forms of God's self-communciation to creation and humankind. Faith and religion can and must be worked out in both the sacral world and in the secular world. One can enter into contact with God equally in either realm. Hence it is clear that secularization is not opposed to religion and to faith, but rather should be understood as opposed to sacralization. Secularization is a different way of living out our faith and our relationship with God. (VSE)

One who professes God but is aloof from justice, who believes in God but does not create bonds of kinship, is not professing or believing in the true God, but in an idol. (FE)

The kingdom of God is not wholly a utopia lying in the future. It is a present reality that finds concrete embodiments in history. It must be viewed as a process that begins in this world and reaches its culmination in the eschatological future. (JCL)

Faith is not concerned only with those things that are called spiritual and supernatural; it also values those that are material and historical. They all belong to the same single enterprise of incarnation whereby the divine permeates the human and the human enters into the divine. (LP)

Historical liberations are not only historical. They are sacraments of a salvation — that is, of a full liberation still in process and present as promise — definitively present in the life, death, and Resurrection of Jesus Christ. Salvation is not identifiable *with* historical liberations, because the latter are always fragmentary, never full. But salvation is identifiable *in* historical liberations introduced by human beings. That is, salvation is concretized, manifested, and anticipated in these historical liberations. (WTLP)

The resurrection is happening; it is a process now underway. Has a heart opened up to another heart in love and forgiveness? The resurrection has been happening there! Have human beings created more just and familial relations among themselves? Resurrection has been taking shape there! Has there been some growth in life, particularly among the oppressed and the wretched? Resurrection has been made manifest there! Has someone died after a good life or in sacrifice for the sake of his or her brothers and sisters? Resurrection has been fully set in motion there! (VSR)

Liberation theologians do not deny any dogma. In doctrinal terms they are rather traditional. Their approach is to invoke the light of the gospel truth and also of dogma, in order to draw the social consequences on behalf of the oppressed who have always been shunted aside in history. The fundamental question is that of the poor. Those who combat us in the church have a hard time accepting that the poor are central in the process of revelation and salvation. They are scandalized to hear that the poor are God's favorites by the very fact of being poor and not because they are good. God is the God of life, and always takes the side of those whose life is threatened or who are forced to die before their time. That is what happens with the poor. Hence the God of liberation is the God of the poor and the outcast. God always hears their cry, from the cry of the oppressed in Egypt to Jesus' desperate cry on the cross. (FB)

The Most Holy Mystery
of God

Faced with the awesome mystery of trinitarian communion, we should be silent. But we can be silent only after trying to speak as adequately as possible of that reality which no human words can properly express. Let us be silent at the end and not at the beginning. Only at the end is silence worthy and holy. At the beginning it would be prejudicial and irreverent. (TS)

God is thus life, love, superabounding communication into which we ourselves are plunged. This vision of mystery does not cause us anguish but opens up our hearts. The Blessed Trinity is mystery now, and will be so for all eternity. We will know it more and more, without ever exhausting our desire to know and to rejoice in the knowledge that we continually acquire. We know in order to sing, we sing in order to love, we love in order to be together in communion with the divine persons, Father, Son, and Holy Spirit. (STMC)

God is the Father, the Son, and the Holy Spirit in reciprocal communion. They coexist from all eternity; none is prior or subsequent, none higher or lower than the other. Each person encompasses the others, and all mutually interpenetrate each other and live in one another. This is the reality of trinitarian communion, so infinite and deep that the divine Three are united and are therefore one sole God. The divine unity is communitarian, since each person is in communion with the other two. (STMC)

If there is a logic within the Blessed Trinity, here it is: to give, give, and give again. The three persons are distinct so as to be able to give themselves to one another. And this giving of themselves is so perfect that the three persons unite and are one sole God. (STMC)

The ultimate principle of the world is not a solitary being, then, but God the Family—God-communion. From all eternity, Yahweh is a bond of loving relations, an unfathomable Mystery—the unoriginated origin of all—called "Father." This Mother and Father emerges from the depths of the divine mystery in an act of self-communication and self-revelation within the Godhead itself, and this emergence is the second person of God: "God the Son." Now Parent and Child—"Father and Son"—join in an embrace of love and in doing so express and give origin to the Holy Spirit, who is the oneness of the first and second persons. This Trinity has not remained enclosed but has communicated itself, making human life its temple. The Trinity dwells in us and our history, divinizing each of us. (FE)

We must Christianize our understanding of God. God is always the communion of the three divine persons. God the Father is never without God the Son and God the Holy Spirit. It is not enough to profess that Jesus is God. It is important to say that Jesus is God, the Son of the Father, together with the Holy Spirit. We cannot speak of one person without also speaking of the other two. (STMC)

The God who is ontologically far away (holy) becomes ethically close (holy): God aids the forsaken, wants to be the vengeance of the oppressed, is identified with the poor. God overcomes the abyss standing between God's own holy reality and our profane reality. God emerges from the inaccessible divine light and penetrates our darkness. The incarnation of the eternal Son embodies in history this tender feeling God has for God's creatures. (LP)

God is purely and simply the living One. Rightly has the concept of life — which humans consider the highest and richest of concepts — been attributed to God. So the supreme goal of human life is represented as sharing in divine life (cf. 1 Pet 1:4). (TS)

In order to be fully human, the human person must relate in three directions: above, alongside, and within. This is the very way the Trinity comes to meet us: the Father is the infinite "above," the Son is the radical "alongside," and the Spirit is the complete "within." (STMC)

Reflective thought never has the first word. First comes life, celebrating life, and work — then comes thinking and doctrine. That is how it was with the early Christians. They began by praising the Father, the Son, and the Holy Spirit. Next they began to baptize persons in the name of the Trinity. Only then did they finally begin to reflect on what they were celebrating and doing. (STMC)

The biblical God is not an idol decorating our churches and the shrines in our homes. This is a living God, whose true name is Justice, Holiness, and Mercy for those who are unjustly oppressed. This is a God who takes the side of Lazarus in the parable — the man who ends up in the bosom of Abraham as opposed to the wealthy glutton who suffers in hell (Lk 16:19–31). This is a God who says, "Blessed are the poor, and those who hunger and thirst for justice, and so are persecuted, cursed, or killed." (FE)

God is not indifferent to crime, to the negative weight in the balance of history. God does not allow the wound to fester until the manifestation of justice at the end of the world. God intervenes and justifies, in the risen Jesus, all the impoverished and crucified of history. The meaning of the resurrection is that justice and love, and the struggles waged for both, have meaning. Their future is guaranteed. Justice, love, and our struggles to attain them only appear to have failed in the process of history. They shall triumph. Good, and good alone, shall reign. (PCPW)

Two divine missions take place in Mary: that of the Holy Spirit who descends upon her, and that of the Son who begins to exist incarnate in her womb. At one moment in history, the Annunciation, she suddenly becomes the center of God's plan and the never-surpassed apex of human ascent toward divinization. (AM)

God does not love as a result of human merit, beauty, or goodness, but simply because that is God's own innermost way of being. God is gratuitous love: God's kindness toward all, even toward the ungrateful and the wicked, is in the form of gift or grace (Lk 6:35). (LG)

The natural desire to love God is not merely human exigency. It is the call that God places within human beings. They hear that call and cry out for God. The cry of human beings is merely an echo of God's voice calling them. (LG)

The universe is pregnant with the mystery of the Blessed Trinity, so close that we do not even notice, so transcendent that it overflows us on all sides, so interior that it dwells in the depths of our heart, so real that it persists despite all sin and all its evil effects. (STMC)

God does not enter the picture directly as something that is part of the world. God comes in as the principle and foundation that makes everything possible. (LG)

It is most reassuring to discover that the Father is only fully Father when he is also present as Mother. As the father of the prodigal son, God awaits us, peering toward the bend in the road, ready to come out to greet us, embrace us, and cover us with kisses. But for this to take place it is important that we yearn for our father's and mother's house and decide to return. (STMC)

If God is in all things, then each being possesses its meaning insofar as it reveals and points toward God. Everything is for God. The greatness and essence of all things is to be a bridge, to be a precursor of the goal, which is God.

When we love a person, we love something more than the person. We love the secret that that person conceals and reveals. Therefore all true love transcends the person loved. The person is the bridge toward the secret that the person incarnates but which also surpasses the person. Love is only happy when the result is that the two who love each other are journeying together in the same direction, the direction indicated by love. Then they are headed toward God, as toward that ineffable secret that lies hidden in everything around us. (VAM)

Consecration certainly involves the idea of being completely set aside for God. However, God is not a being who needs persons and things. God is infinite and self-sufficient, and is in need of nothing. If someone is set aside for God by being consecrated, that person is sent back into the world in God's name. It is not God, but the world that needs salvation and the means for making it active and visible. Being consecrated and being set aside inherently entail mission in the world in God's name. To be religious means being taken out of the world in order to be sent into the world more deeply, with a specific mission: to make present a world that is reconciled and no longer shot through with alienation, rebelliousness, and sin. (VSE)

More important than being aware of the good is doing good. More important than knowing how the Father, the Son, and the Holy Spirit are one sole God is living the communion that is the essence of the Trinity. (STMC)

How many nights in bed have I not asked, "What is God like; what term expresses the communion of the divine three?" And no word have I found, nor has any insight come to me. Then I have begun to praise and glorify. That is when my heart has swelled with light. I was no longer raising questions; I was standing within the divine communion itself. (STMC)

This whole universe, all these stars above our heads, these woods, these birds, these insects, these rivers and these rocks, everything, everything is going to be preserved, transfigured, and made a temple of the Blessed Trinity. And we will live in a magnificent house, as in one family: minerals, vegetables, animals, and humans with the Father, the Son, and the Holy Spirit. Amen. (STMC)

Jesus, Root Sacrament
of God

When looking at Jesus Christ we can truly say: The mystery of human beings evokes the mystery of God; living out the mystery of God evokes the mystery of human beings. We cannot speak of human beings without having to speak of God and we cannot speak of God without speaking of human beings ... The more Jesus presents himself as a human person the more God is manifested; the more divine Jesus is, the more the human person is revealed. (JCL)

Jesus Christ is the encounter between the human being seeking God and God seeking the human being. He is the crossroads where God's descending road and humankind's ascending road meet. (EHJ)

We are so tired of hearing and saying "the Word became flesh" that we do not stop to think what this means. He really wanted to become one of us, like me and you, in everything but sin: a limited man who grows, learns, and questions; a man who can listen and answer. God did not assume an abstract humanity, a "rational animal." From the very moment of conception, God took on a being in history, Jesus of Nazareth, a Jew by both race and religion, who was shaped in the confines of his mother's womb; who grew up in the confines of a minor country, and came to maturity

in the confines of a small village out in the countryside;
who worked in limited and not very intellectual surround-
ings; who knew neither Greek nor Latin, the main languages
at that time, but spoke Aramaic with a Galilean accent;
who felt the oppression of the occupation forces in his country; who experienced hunger, thirst, and longing; who shed
tears over the death of a friend; who felt the joy of friendship, sadness, fear, temptations, and the horror of death;
and who went through the dark night of being abandoned
by God. All this God assumed in Jesus Christ, and was
spared nothing. God assumed everything that is truly human
and belongs to our condition, like just anger and healthy
rejoicing, kindness and harshness, friendship and conflict,
life and death. All this is present in the frail figure of the
child who starts whining in the manger between the ox and
the ass. (EHJ)

The Incarnation contains a message that concerns not
only Jesus Christ but also the nature and destiny of every
person. By means of the Incarnation we come to know who
in fact we are and what we are destined for. We come to
know the nature of God, who in Jesus Christ comes to our
encounter with a face like ours — respecting our otherness —
in order to assume human nature and fill it with his divine
reality. (JCL)

The resurrection of the crucified one shows that to die as
Jesus died, for others and for God, is not without meaning.
The anonymous death of all the vanquished of history, for
justice' sake — for the sake of openness and ultimate meaning in human life — finds its explanation in Jesus' resurrection. The resurrection delivers us from history's most blatant
absurdity: the sacrifice of one's life in anonymity. (FE)

The discipleship of the historical Jesus is an attempt to implement Project Human Being in everyone alive — and in the ambiguity of a Project Human Being that must be realized in the presence of Project Nonhuman Being. (FE)

The universal meaning of the life and death of Christ is that he sustained the fundamental conflict of human existence to the end: he wanted to realize the absolute meaning of this world before God, in spite of hate, incomprehension, betrayal, and condemnation to death. For Jesus, evil does not exist in order to be comprehended, but to be taken over and conquered by love. This comportment of Jesus opened up a new possibility for human existence — that is, an existence of faith with absolute meaning, even when confronted with the absurd, as was his own death — caused by hate for one who only loved and only sought to do good among people. (JCL)

Jesus detheologizes religion, making people search for the will of God not only in holy books but principally in daily life; he demythologizes religious language, using the expressions of our common experiences; he deritualized piety, insisting that one is always before God and not only when one goes to the temple to pray; he emancipates the message of God from its connection to one religious community and directs it to all people of good will; and, finally, he secularizes the means of salvation, making the sacrament of the "other" a determining element for entry into the kingdom of God. (JCL)

Jesus did not seek death; it was imposed on him from without. Nor did he accept it with resignation. He accepted it as an expression of his freedom and fidelity to the cause of God and human beings. (FE)

Jesus died for the reasons any prophet ever dies. He placed a higher value on the principles he preached than on his own life. (PCPW)

Jesus is not alone on the cross. His followers are there. They take on his cause, imitate his life, and follow out his fate. (FA)

Facing Jesus, the believer is facing God and the *ecce homo* in all its starkness. The man-Jesus is not the external receptacle for God, as though a fragile glass were receiving God as a precious essence. The man-Jesus is God's very self when God comes into the world and makes history: "And the Word *became* human condition and set up his tent among us" (Jn 1:14). God experiences a *becoming*, without losing anything of God's being. When God *becomes* and turns into unfolding and history, it is right there that the one we call Jesus Christ, Word incarnate, emerges. Most Christians have still not gotten used to this idea. (JCL)

What is properly redemptive in Jesus is neither the cross, nor blood, nor death, taken by themselves. It is rather his stance of love, surrender, and forgiveness. (CPCH)

Christ's death, even apart from the light bestowed upon it in his resurrection, has a meaning consistent with his life. All who, like Jesus, demand more justice, more love, more respect for the rights of the oppressed, and more liberty for God, must expect opposition, and the possibility of their liquidation. Death is vanquished when it ceases to be the terrifying specter that prevents us from living and proclaiming the truth. Now death is accepted. It is simply inserted into the project of the just person and true prophet. It can be expected. It must be expected. (PCPW)

Being *against* is not what defines Christ; he is not a complainer. He is *in favor* of love, justice, reconciliation, hope, and the complete fulfillment of the meaning of human existence in God. If he is *against*, it is because he first takes a stand *in favor*. (JCL)

Jesus Christ did not merely teach some truths. He journeyed on a path in which he assumed the whole of life, both its positive and negative features, as a life lived, endured, and assumed vis-à-vis God and always with God as the starting point. (TCL)

Even the most divine titles and names are not intended to obscure the man Jesus but indeed to highlight him. They do not seek to demonstrate the sovereignty and authority of Jesus, but to express it and bring it into prominence. Ultimately, after a long process of meditation on the mystery hidden in Jesus, people came to the point of saying: A human being such as Jesus of Nazareth was in his life, death, and resurrection can only be God himself. And so they called him God. (JCL)

Only when taken in conjunction with his life and death does Jesus' resurrection have a realistic meaning. Otherwise it becomes either pagan mythology, or a modern ideology of a future of reconciliation without the conversion of historical evils. In Jesus, resurrection means the victory of life, the victory of the rights of the oppressed, the victory of justice for the weak. (PCPW)

To follow Jesus is to pursue his work, further his cause, and thereby attain to his fullness. (FE)

Christ demands basically two things: conversion of the person and a restructuring of the person's world. (JCL)

The cross is a human invention. It was devised in order to torture the bodies of prophets and injure the bodily members that engage in liberating practice: the hands, feet, and heart. The cross is a tool of oppression.

But it is also blessing. Jesus embraced the cross in order to be lord over the suffering and death produced by contempt. That is why he wanted to be in solidarity with — or better yet, be identified with — history's crucified ones. Never again will they die alone. Jesus dies crucified along with them. (FA)

Christ emerges as the root sacrament of God, and his community becomes the radical sacrament of Christ. The church ought to be the sign of universal grace and of God's boundless love in the world. It ought to be the sacrament of the unheard of hope embodied in the resurrection, and of the joy of living in the Father's world, linked in kinship with all creatures, and secure at home among brothers and sisters. (LG)

To declare Jesus of Nazareth to be the Christ is to profess utopia to have become *topos*. To declare Jesus of Nazareth to be the Christ is to use the eschatological symbol of the Christ, the Messiah, to testify that, amidst this old world and these sinful human beings, a new world is in ferment. A leaven is at work in the dough. Jesus Christ is already free. One of our number is totally liberated — free at last. (FE)

Prayer: Experience of God

Prayer translates the highest expression of living faith. Through prayer the person leaves behind, as it were, the universe of all things and seeks a relationship with God. Here we have the manifestation of true human transcendence. Only human beings can take up an "ecstatic" position, in other words, contemplate God face to face, cry out, "My Father," and so get beyond all the limits imposed by creation and history. In this stance humans find their supreme dignity. To pray is an act of courage; it presumes greatness and expansiveness of spirit and heart beyond the boundless time and open space of the vast cosmos. (AM)

Prayer is not the first thing that a person does. Before praying, one experiences an existential shock. Only then does prayer pour forth, whether in the form of supplication, or of an act of thanksgiving, or of worship. (LP)

Through prayer human beings express what is noblest and deepest in their existence: they can rise above themselves, transcend all the wonders of creation and history, assume an "ecstatic" stance, and establish a dialogue with the supreme mystery, and shout: Father! When they do so they are not leaving the universe behind, but rather assuming it and transforming it into an offering to God. They are, moreover, freeing themselves from all chains, denouncing all historical absolutes, relativizing them, and in solitude and nakedness confronting the absolute, in order to forge history together with that absolute. (VSE)

The Lord's Prayer deals with the major themes of the personal and social existence of all humankind in every era. There is no reference here to the church, not even a word about Jesus, his death, or his resurrection. God is at the center of the stage, where the other center — that of humanity and its needs — converges. (LP)

To pray "thy will be done" is equivalent to saying: let what God wants be done! There is no element of complaint or despair in this, but a confident commitment, like that of a child snuggling into the arms of its mother. God is Father and Mother of infinite goodness. God has an eternal plan; all we have is what we intend to do. (LP)

If we want to be united to the Blessed Trinity we ought to follow the same route as Jesus: pray with familiar intimacy, act radically in the direction of justice and communion, and accept our own death as a form of utter surrender and ultimate communion, even with our enemies. (STMC)

From the Christian standpoint, all true liberation arises out of a deep encounter with God, which impels us toward committed action. (LP)

We are not sanctifying the name of God when we erect church buildings, when we elaborate mystical treatises, or when we guarantee his official presence in society by means of religious symbols. His holy name is sanctified only to the extent that these expressions are related to a pure heart, a thirst for justice, and a reaching out for perfection. It is in these realities that God dwells; these are his true temples, where there are no idols. (LP)

Francis was a deeply sacramental person in the sense that he intuitively produced gestures, symbols, and meaningful actions. His own underlying notion of following Christ

tended toward presenting and dramatizing the life and attitudes of the historic Jesus. Celebration of faith is not limited just to liturgical celebrations. He did not pray, like monks, only within some sacred space; his experience of God took place in the world, in contact with people, with the poor, and with nature. The various prayers he left us evidence his deep spiritual creativity. In his sermons "he used simple material comparisons . . . and he swayed his listeners with fiery gestures and expressions." Stories about him are full of the language of deeds, whether he is dressing like a beggar and pleading for alms in French, having himself led through the streets in his underwear and shouting, "Look at the glutton who claims to be a brother in penance," or dancing in a pilgrim's outfit on Easter, or putting ashes on his head or in his food to offer his brethren a lesson in humility. He celebrates life as a liturgy since in all things he detects traces of God, of Christ, or passages of the gospels. The "Canticle to Brother Sun" shows this new sense of prayer in contact with life and its dramas. (SF)

Church of Heaven
and Earth

The church is rooted in faith. Dogmas, rituals, formulas, and canons do not produce faith. Rather it is faith that produces canons, formulas, rituals, and dogmas, and is expressed in them. Normally, it is not miracles that produce faith; it is faith that produces miracles. (DHM)

Christianity asserts that it is not the fate of the human being to remain forever a Prometheus, or a Sisyphus unendingly hauling a boulder up to a height that is never reached. The human being is not called to accept an eternal return to a zero point, nor to remain devoured by thirst for an unattainable omega. Human beings will not remain nailed to the cross forever, nor is their homeland the grave. (DHM)

The Church is that part of the world that, in the strength of the Spirit, has accepted the Kingdom made explicit in the person of Jesus Christ, the Son of God incarnated in oppression. It preserves the constant memory and consciousness of the Kingdom, celebrating its presence in the world, shaping the way it is proclaimed, and at the service of the world. The Church is not the Kingdom but rather its sign (explicit symbol) and its instrument (mediation) in the world. (CCP)

If the church as a great, united whole is one big sacrament, then so are all the things in it. All the things in the church are sacramental because they recall Christ or give concreteness to the church as sacrament: the liturgy with its rites, sacred objects, books, and material elements; the people, from the pope down to the lowliest member; the activity of the church in the world, including social assistance, missionary work, and prophetic proclamation. In the eyes of the church fathers, even the dismissal of a bishop and the profession of a religious were considered sacramental. All the gestures, acts, and words of the church-sacrament likewise assume a sacramental function: they are spelling out in life what the church-as-sacrament is all about. (SL)

As the fontal sacrament, Christ was human and divine, so in an analogous way the universal sacrament, the church, is also human and divine. (It is not so in exactly the same way because there is no hypostatic union in the church.) The divine element is always incarnated in the human element, making the latter transparent. The human element is in the service of the divine element, making the latter historical. Thus, the church is really more a living organism than an organization, a community of salvation rather than an institution of salvation. (SL)

Christianity sees itself, not primarily as an architectonic system of saving truths, but rather as the communication of divine life within this world. The world, things, and human beings have come to be penetrated by the generous sap of God. Things are bearers of salvation and a mystery. That is why they are sacramental. To a large extent, Christian opposition to Marxism is due to its different understanding of matter. Christianity says that matter is not merely an object for human manipulation and possession. It is a bearer of God and a place where we encounter salvation. Matter is sacramental. (SL)

The church is the locus in which this total salvation becomes awareness, proclamation, and celebration. Transcending the division of society into oppressed and oppressor, transcending historical struggles, the church offers to all the opportunity for God's reconciliation and presents an *eschaton* already realized in the earthly journey of Jesus who lived, died, and was raised from the dead. (FE)

Christian faith is true only if, as God does in the incarnation, it continually takes on what differs from it—the world, what is most adverse—and reconciles and reunifies with it in forgiveness and mercy. Then the other becomes like us, and what is like us becomes our neighbor. (TCL)

God's judgment begins at home (1 Peter 4:17)—that is, with the church. Many of the crises within it are really God's judgments over its lack of fidelity and openness to the newness of the Spirit. (VAM)

When the church forgets the source from which it was born—the community of the three divine persons—it allows its unity to be turned into uniformity, and one group of believers assumes all responsibilities by itself, thus making it difficult for others to participate; it allows its own confessional interests to prevail over the interests of God's reign. In short, the river of crystalline waters is in danger of becoming a stagnant pond. Being converted to the Trinity is important for recovering the diversity and communion that create the kind of dynamic unity that is ever open to being enriched in new ways. (STMC)

Behind every innovative practice in the church, and at the root of every genuine and genuinely new theology, is a latent religious experience. This total existential experience, this "word," is the source from which all else springs. The rest is an effort to translate this word into the framework of a particular situation in history. (FE)

What the popular church generates is not division but a new vision of church. The basic feature of this vision is that it connects the discourse of gospel faith with the discourse of society. It is a different model of church and hence it leads to tension with the other church, which is more sacramental, more devotional, more connected to the dominant classes. Nevertheless, I think it is possible to live out this tension together and in peace within one and the same church. (*IstoÉ*, June 1983)

We must surely help the church avoid becoming a small bastion of machismo and clerical domination, claiming to hold a monopoly over salvation. Rather, it should be a space where humankind feels even more human because it finds further energy for its own aspirations and finds a place where it can nourish its dreams of a world that is ultimately reconciled to itself and to nature. (FB)

The church does not live just off its Petrine quality — that is, the tradition and structure of sacramental power. It also lives off its Pauline quality, its charismatic creativity, its new response to the challenges posed by the pagans of yesterday and today. Charism and power make up the two poles on the basis of which the ellipse of the church is built. Currently the Petrine dimension, that of orders and canon law, is being inflated and made an instrument for forcing the

whole church into a neo-Romanization and into a kind of
discipline that ignores communion, while safeguarding clerical privilege, since it understands communion simply as a
one-way street from lay person to priest, priest to bishop,
and bishop to pope, with no return route of any sort. (FB)

Neither Paul nor John fell into a doctrinal fixation, alleg-
ing that such and such words were actually spoken by the
Word of life but rather, with a basic fidelity to the spirit of
Christ and his message, they translated those words into
concepts and expressions that their hearers could understand, accept, and thus be converted to faith in Jesus Christ
the savior. The same can be said about ecclesiastical institutions. Only if they are open to an ongoing perfection,
reform, and adaptation will they be of service to the Spirit
in the church and in the world. Otherwise, they run the
risk of becoming conservative and an oppressive power contrary to the liberating development of grace and faith.
(CCP)

When they gather as church, the people have a right to
remain as a people while retaining all their own values.
Their store of symbols ought to constitute the matter for
liturgical prayer; their creativity in ritual ought to be assured
of citizenship within the church's official prayer. (FE)

The community has a right to receive the faith of the
apostles, which is by that very fact orthodox, but it also has
a right to receive it in a contemporary expression — namely,
in terms of the culture that is familiar to the community.
The effort to serve in this manner entails taking on the risks
inherent in all processes of discovering and working out
meaning. Error should not be seen as an utter disaster, but

as a moment in the overall process of fidelity to the faith. It can enable us to learn by engaging in critical examination and correcting our course. (IFP)

Dogma is one thing and dogmatism quite another, law versus legalism, tradition versus traditionalism, authority versus authoritarianism. Christianity was reduced, in its pathological Catholic understanding, to a simple doctrine of salvation: it became more important to know the truths "required for salvation" than to be converted to a praxis of following Jesus Christ. Jesus is adored, as are his Holy Land, his words, his history; saints are venerated; martyrs are praised, heroic witness to faith is celebrated; but the principal element is missing: following them and doing what they did. (CCP)

I can see that during these last few years the church has traveled along a wonderful road. At first only the priests came to meetings; then it was the priests and those doing pastoral work, and soon it was priests, church workers, the women who were leading communities, and finally it was the priests, church workers, the women, and representatives from the people who were living out their faith in their communities. Our thinking became socialized as a result of a growing awareness that we are a single people of God, and that in practice we work together in an organized collegial way. Collegiality is a feature not just of bishops' conferences, but of the whole of God's people. (FB)

The Sacrament of the Poor

The Gospels ascribe to the poor an altogether special privilege. Their poverty and marginality, being the fruit of injustice, constitutes a challenge to the messianic king. The Reign of God, as the actualization of right order and the reestablishment of the right of the humiliated and the wronged, begins with them. The poor have a sacramental function. They provide the rest of us with an opportunity to encounter the Lord, who is concealed in them anonymously. Their longings for liberation and their thirst for justice have been taken up by the "Son of Man." Whenever the Church takes sides with the impoverished, then, the Church is infallible, since it thereby establishes and proclaims its presence in Jesus's own social locus, where he uttered his proclamation of liberation and then fitted his actions to his declared intent. (FE)

It is God's way to delight in those who are on the bottom and downtrodden. (TEP)

If there is a place for God in this world, it is alongside the poor, those who do not accept their poverty and are organizing in solidarity to overcome poverty ... God wants neither rich nor poor, but people who work and who live in solidarity and justice. That is why Marxism has helped us understand that the poor are not simply poor but oppressed, and that this oppression is the product of a process of the exploitation of labor by capital . . . Poverty is not innocent, not produced by nature, not what God wants. It is the result of a process that produces wealth and poverty side by side. (*La Juventud* [Cono Sur Press], November 1987)

The community born of faith in Christ and in his Spirit (church of the resurrection) must accept, and be in communion with, the church that is real in the poor (church of the crucifixion). And this communion is only true if it obeys Christ's appeal in the poor: "I was naked, I was hungry, I was jailed, and you freed me, you fed me, and you clothed me!" For the first time in history, the poor become important as church and not simply as objects of charity. (SF)

To accept a poor person as poor is to accept the poor Jesus. He hides himself, he is incognito, behind each human face. Faith demands that we look profoundly into the face of our brothers and sisters; love them; give them food, drink, and clothing; visit them in prison. For in so doing, we are being host to and serving Christ himself. Hence the human being is the greatest manifestation not only of God, but also of Christ resurrected in our world. Whoever rejects his brother or sister rejects Christ himself, because whoever rejects the image and likeness of God and Christ rejects God and Christ himself (cf. Gen 9:6; Matt 25:42–43). Without the sacrament of brother and sister, no one can be saved. Here the identification of love of neighbor and love of God becomes transparent. (JCL)

The eucharist cannot be celebrated in the spirit of Jesus when that celebration is unaccompanied by a hunger and thirst for justice. We betray the eucharist, the memorial of the Lord, when we utilize it for the concealment of, or even when we merely ignore, the presence of unjust relations in the community of the faithful who celebrate and assist at that eucharist. (FE)

Indeed, the great and truly salvific sacrament is the sacrament of the poor. When we enter into communion through solidarity and the love that takes care of their needs, we are infallibly entering into communion with Christ who is hidden in them and identified with them. (WTLP)

Jesus' practice initiates the reign because it is a practice of communion with the poor, of reconciliation with sinners, of living in common with all, especially the outcast, and of serving everyone he meets without exception. (TS)

When read from the perspective of the poor, the gospel takes on new vigor. Only there is it really understood as good news of hope and liberation for the poor. The cross of Christ is not a statement piously dwelling on pain; it is everyday reality. The resurrection takes on new dimensions for it becomes clear that where people are becoming aware of their dignity, getting organized, and coming to a sense of community and common endeavor, life is winning out, right is beginning to prevail, and justice is starting to come about. (VSE)

A preferential option for the poor comes down to this: someone who is not poor becomes poor, in order to identify with the poor and together with them overcome their poverty—and thus to move, all together, in the direction of justice and a communion of sisters and brothers. (WTLP)

So long as there is no conversion of the oppressed and the oppressors, peace cannot be more than mere pacification. Pacification is not tranquility based on order; it is tranquility within a context of disorder that is imposed by the violence of the stronger over the weaker. That is not the peace of God nor the peace brought by Jesus Christ. To achieve the peace that is the fruit of justice, we must struggle to overcome the objective causes of divisiveness and injustice. It is the justice of this cause that determines the rightness of the struggle. Living in peace with God and other human beings, the graced person fights on with a new sense of purpose and without a spirit of vengeance. This is a form of love motivated by justice, and it is the real matrix of any authentic or lasting peace. To experience that profound peace which the world can neither give nor take away (John 14:27) is to experience the grace of God pervading one's heart and the world. (LG)

What makes poverty inhumane is not just the failure to minimally satisfy basic needs. It is the contempt, the rejection, the sense of being left out of common human life, the fact that the poor themselves are continually taking in a negative, contemptuous image shaped by the nonpoor classes. Poor people end up believing they are miserable and contemptible. No one stands up for them; their own fortune in life and other people are all against them. (SF)

The poor are there not because of some inevitable fate; their existence is not politically neutral nor is it ethically innocent. The poor person is the by-product of the system in which we live and for which we are responsible. The poor person is actually someone who has been impoverished, someone plundered, robbed, and defrauded of the fruit of his or her labor and dignity. Such impoverishment generates an appeal for Christian love, not simply to relieve the demeaning burden of poverty, but to create conditions for overcoming this situation. (TCL)

In Latin America the poverty of millions of people should certainly goad us into thinking about liberation as a way of overcoming the things causing this poverty. These causes are not a matter of lack of bread. Rather they lie in the system of ownership that prevents millions from having access to dignified work and from taking part in the life of society. It is here that theological reflection and the practice of faith should focus. (TCL)

Solidarity with the poor for the sake of the gospel leads members of religious orders to break with a kind of life and relationships characteristic of those who are well-off in society. Their presence in the world becomes a critical and prophetic sign. The poor with whom they stand in solidarity are not simply poor: they are impoverished, those whose means for being members of society have been taken away, and who have been shoved off to one side. An intelligent love for the poor makes it imperative to come to a deep understanding of the social structure that causes poverty as a by-product of the wealth of the well-off minorities. Hence the need for religious to be critical rather than naive, and to always be alert to the way the status quo can manipulatively take advantage of the religious life by encouraging it to engage in a kind of aid that tranquilizes people's consciences and creates the illusion that religious are providing true service to the world of the poor. The critical presence of religious means denouncing a situation that contradicts God's plan and the gospel message and proclaiming true fellowship and the sharing of those goods and the burdens that all should bear. (TCL)

The church's option is a preferential option *for the poor, against their poverty.* The "poor" here are those who suffer injustice. Their poverty is produced by mechanisms of impoverishment and exploitation. Their poverty is an evil and an injustice. An option for the poor implies a choice for social justice. It means a commitment to the poor in the transformation of society and the elimination of unjust poverty. It means a struggle for a society of more justice and greater partnership. (FE)

To me being a Franciscan means the challenge to be simple in order to encounter God on earth, in my brother or sister, especially in the poor, and in being faithful to the blood and to the earthly roots of our existence, which has been visited by God's Son, who became our brother in all of this and despite all of this. (*Jornal de Petrópolis*, July 1980)

The Human Being
as Parable of God

What are human beings? Misery and grandeur. And their grandeur is all the more marvelous insofar as it arises out of their very misery. It arises basically as an open-ended questioning. It is yearning for fullness, an infinite longing, and a crying out into the vast empty spaces. Who will answer? Human beings seek the infinite and yet encounter only finite beings. They seek an absolute love and only come across attempts that further frustrate their searching. Deep down, what is the aim of the human being? To be like God: full, absolute, eternal, infinitely fulfilled. Is this utopia going to come about? Will the tireless human heart be stilled? (EHJ)

The human being is a parable of God. If humans are communion, transcendence, openness to others, it is because in the realm of creatures they reproduce God's very own way of being. (EHJ)

The word *road* sums up one of the deepest experiences of human beings as they confront the task of life. Life is never a given—it is always a task—something that must be done and carried out. We do not live simply by not dying. We walk toward life. To live is to walk. Walking assumes that there is a road. (VSE)

The person as mystery, intelligence, and love, constitutes a dynamic and ever-open unity. These are not three things thrown together. It is always the person who is mystery, who thinks, and who loves. Thus each one of us in our unity and our diversity shows that we are really image and likeness of God, who is Father, Son, and Holy Spirit. How respectfully we should treat each person, since she or he is a temple of the Blessed Trinity! (STMC)

The human being is a knot of relationships and throbbings in all directions. Humans are not focused on this or that object but on the totality of objects. Hence they are forever abandoning anything stuck and limited, and they are always protesting and challenging closed worlds. What lies within them is not simply being, but being-able-to-be. They are projection and striving toward an ever-more, toward an unknown, toward the novum and the not-yet. (FE)

Humans are beings who can read the world's message. They are never illiterate with respect to this particular alphabet. They can read and interpret the message in a multiplicity of languages. To live is to read and interpret. In the ephemeral, they can read the permanent; in the temporal, the eternal; in the world, God. The ephemeral is thereby transfigured into a sign of the presence of the permanent, the temporal into a symbol of the reality of the eternal, and the world into a magnificent sacrament of God. (SL)

When through God's gracious will human beings so open up in this way and accept supreme love as the fullness of their infinite emptiness, when human beings are so united to God, through God's very power and grace to the point of becoming one with God, then we can say that humans reach their utter humanization and also attain to divinization. (EHJ)

All life is sacred and points back to a most holy mystery. Hence every assault against life is nothing less than an aggression against God. (EHJ)

The basic starting point for my anthropology is the not-human, the human being who is nullified, humiliated, oppressed. This not-human must be liberated and must become the new person as in the biblical revelation. So I call it a prophetic anthropology, because it condemns what almost all anthropological systems have been talking about until the present, the human being who conquers, who wins, the transcendent human being ... The starting point has changed: an anthropology from below is different from a top-down anthropology. (*Jesus* [Italy], February 1985)

Christ did not come to found a new religion. He came to bring a new human being, one who is defined not by the established criteria of society, but by the option for the cause of love, which is the cause of Christ. (JCL)

In praying the Lord's Prayer, the Christian's gaze should not be directed backward in search of an ancestral past, but forward, in the direction of the advent of that kingdom promised by the Father, which is above, in heaven. The forward look and the upward look depict the attitude of hope and of faith in the love that rejoices with God the Father who is near, while also loving the Father-God who is far away. This attitude is neither alienating nor dehumanizing. It puts us in our proper place of greatness as sons and daughters in the presence of a beloved Father. (LP)

Life is ontologically mortal. Death does not suddenly appear on the scene at the close of our life. It installs itself at life's very heart. We die continuously. We waste away, spending our vital energy, consuming each minute of life until our dying is done. We die not only because someone kills us. Life hosts death in its own very structure. (WTLP)

Death is certainly the end of life — end, however, understood as reaching the goal, the fullness for which we yearn, and where we are truly born. The union that is interrupted by this ending is but the prelude to a more intimate and more comprehensive communion. (VAM)

Inside a great saint there always coexists a great demon. The roots of sanctity are born in the depths of human frailty. Virtues are great because the temptations overcome were great. Holiness is not imbibed like mother's milk. Beneath the saint there lies a human being who knew the infernal depths of human nature and the vertigo of sin, despair, and the denial of God. Like Jacob, the saint has struggled with God (Gen 23), and that combat has left its mark. Hence to imagine the life of a saint carefree, easy, and clear-cut reflects naivety and ignorance. Holiness is the reward of arduous conquest. (SF)

The most fearful and unbearable feeling is rejection and knowing that we are not accepted. And to feel ill at ease in our nest is to experience psychological death. When we say "Father" we mean to express this conviction: there is someone who accepts me absolutely; my moral situation matters little, I can always trust that there is someone to take me in and embrace me. There I will not be a stranger, but a child, even a prodigal child, in my parent's house. (STMC)

The more deeply human beings relate to the world and to the things of *their own* world, the more clearly sacramentality shows up. Then there emerges the native homeland that is more than the geographical boundaries of a country, the place of our birth that is more than a parcel of government land, the native city that is more than the sum of its houses and inhabitants, the parental home that is more than a stone building. In all those things dwell values, good and evil spirits, and the lineaments of a human landscape. Sacramental thinking means that the roads we travel, the mountains we see, the rivers that bathe our lands, the houses that inhabit our neighborhoods, and the persons that create our society, are not simply people, houses, rivers, mountains, and roads like all the others in the world. They are unique and incomparable. They are a part of ourselves. So we rejoice and suffer over their fate. We lament the felling of the huge tree in our town square or the demolition of an old shed. Something of ourselves dies along with them. Why? Because they are no longer merely things. They are sacraments in our life, be it blessed or cursed. (SL)

While universally valid formulas and methods can be used for the realm of objects, there is no ready-made formula at hand for the world of persons. What we have are suggestions, appeals, calls, guidelines. Hence one cannot reproduce spiritual experiences and turn them out in series as one does scientific experiments. Each individual sees the world with his or her own eyes and makes sense of reality out of a personal core that is irreducible. Even if someone sets out to follow faithfully in the steps of Jesus Christ or Saint Francis, he or she will never turn out like Jesus Christ or Saint Francis. (VSE)

Being a human being is worth the trouble—God wanted to be one. We are not a condemned herd or an anonymous mass set adrift. God does not stand by passively, observing the human tragedy, but enters into it. God becomes involved and reveals God's self to us. It is worth the effort to live life as we experience it: monotonous, anonymous, demanding, and faithful in the struggle to be better every day, demanding in our patience with ourselves and with others, strong in putting up with contradictions, and wise in order to learn from them. The Word of God has taken on all these manifestations of life. (EHJ)

Human beings are the supreme blossoming of the world, and hence they can never deny their earthly roots, even as they transcend them. (VAM)

Toward a New Society

The desire of Christians to create a society of equals — one built on participatory mechanisms for all and respectful of differences, and yet one that prevents differences from becoming inequities — is grounded in the equal dignity of the three divine persons, in their simultaneity and their loving coexistence. (STMC)

Christians who are committed to substantial changes in society in the direction of greater participation by the people can view trinitarian communion as a source of inspiration even more than of critique. In the Trinity no one pole dominates, but rather the three equals in dignity, who are united in communion and mutual self-giving and receiving, converge. A society is a sacrament of the Trinity only when the class barriers within it come tumbling down, some do not dominate others, and all feel, and really are, integrated in a greater whole that is equitable and rich in the expression it allows for personal and community differences. In such a society it is neither euphemism nor figure of speech to call the other person brother or sister. Society truly becomes human with relationships that are humane and express solidarity. (FE)

Would there not be such harmony, joy, and justice in our world if in our thinking and acting we adopted trinitarian logic: ever-inclusive, ever-encompassing, ever-communitarian, ever-accepting of differences and preventing them from becoming inequities! (STMC)

The power of conviction that comes from the so-called popular church is largely the result of the way it develops in Christians the ability to sacrifice their life for others, to accept persecution, torture, and martyrdom in condemning social and structural sin, and in the commitment to bring to birth a more equal, free, and familial society. (IFP)

In the process of struggle, reform and liberation are not at odds. Liberation occurs whenever interpersonal and social relationships are reorganized according to another principle, one of collaboration rather than exploitation. The crucial point is not so much to kick out the agents of oppression but actually to overcome oppressive relationships, which show up in the family, and in the way people treat each other, at work, and in social gatherings. (IFP)

I think that for well-intentioned people this society can no longer represent the future. There is no salvation for the poor in capitalism. In both moral and religious terms we ought to condemn capitalism for generating death rather than life. (*La Juventud* [Cono Sur Press], November 1987)

The real problem in both church and society is not Marxism, but fear of changing. One who opts for the perspective of the poor calls for change, because the situation is so absurd that it can no longer be tolerated. Absolute rejection of Marxism becomes the mask that conceals the refusal to change, whether in society or in the church. (*Jesus* [Italy], February 1985)

Socialism demands that the church be organized in a more participatory way, with a better ecclesiastical division of religious labor, one in which sacred power is also socialized among all community members. This does not mean that there will no longer be bishops and priests, but that they will function differently and will embody a kind of coordination and leadership different from that exercised in the framework of a church viewed as society. (FE)

There is no such thing as an apolitical church, neither in the realm of epistemology nor in that of politics. When Pope Paul VI asked Christians not to vote for a communist candidate, he was acting as a political figure. In other words, when our interests are at stake, the church speaks up and has always spoken up. Anything else is hypocrisy, and untrue. (*Jornal do Brasil*, December 1979)

Neutrality is impossible. We all take stances; it happens that some people have not been conscious of their position. Generally, these people assume the position of the dominant class, of the established order, which in many cases is manifestly antipopular, unequal, and unjust. Attempted apoliticism results in the manipulation and mutilation of the gospel. We need to become more conscious of the political dimension of the gospel and our faith. (CCP)

What hinders encountering others and God is the desire to possess, and vested interests that thrust themselves between persons, dividing them into haves and have-nots. (FA)

There is a kind of life that cannot be devoured by death, one that accepts dying for God, for others, and for the cause of justice to the lowly. (VSR)

God's mercy is not just held in reserve until the end of time. It does not allow the wound to remain open and bleed forever. It assumes particular forms in history and is embodied in deeds that transform the play of forces. The proud, those who rule, and the rich do not have the last word, as they always claim. Divine justice comes down upon them in history. They will be unseated from power; their proud masks will be torn off, and they will be sent away empty-handed. (FE)

Power becomes legitimate to the extent it becomes a means and instrument for right and justice. (FE)

God did not leave us a finished world, but wanted us to join in the task of transformation. Work has its own dignity and holiness, and it needs no baptism of prayer or super-naturalizing good intention. Work is sacred by its own nature as creation set within the Christic project. The supreme value of work is not that it be executed with a right intention, but that it be ordered to building up the earthly city intended by God in anticipation of the heavenly one. (FE)

We don't get anywhere just with slogans. The Christian's commitment is through direct involvement. That means creating ever-more participatory forms in society, and social relations that are more symmetrical, though not utopian. There are always conflicts. Our function is to create a society where it is less difficult to be sisters and brothers to one another—one where love is less difficult. To work in this direction is to help overcome class struggle. And you don't fight the struggle by just being a tranquil observer. (*Journal do Brasil*, December 1979)

The dominant classes are fatalists to some extent because they can only envision the future as the extension, development, and improvement of the framework in which they now stand ... For them the future means an ever-more sophisticated way of getting rich, one whose mechanisms are under their control. So by their very function in history they are fatalistic, enjoying their own present and devoid of any more transcendent sense of the future as the creation of the new, the different . . . The exploited classes, however, who cannot look back to any past . . . have a perverse present. All they have is the future and the changes that will be able to offer them better living conditions. Hence they are the only bearers of hope. (*Diário de Pernambuco*, October 1978)

Human life is indissolubly connected with a material infrastructure. No matter how high the spirit soars, no matter how deep our mystical probings, or how metaphysical our abstract thinking, the human being will always be dependent on a piece of bread, a cup of water — in short, on a handful of matter. (LP)

When the bread that we eat is the result of exploitation, it is not a bread blessed by God. It may supply the chemical needs of nutrition but fail to nourish human life, which is human only when lived within the framework of justice and fellowship. Unjust bread is not really our bread; it is stolen; it belongs to someone else. The great medieval mystic, Meister Eckhart, well said: "They who do not give to another what belongs to the other are not eating their own bread, but are eating both their bread and the other's." (LP)

The Franciscan world is brimming with magic, reverence, and respect. It is not a dead and inanimate universe; things are not tossed here, within the reach of possessive appetites of hunger, nor are they just jumbled together. They have souls and personalities; there are blood ties with humanity; they dwell together in the same parental home. Because they are our sisters and brothers, they cannot be violated but must be respected. Hence it is that Saint Francis, surprisingly, but in a way consistent with his nature, forbade his brethren to cut the trees down by the root, with the hope that they might bud again. He told the gardeners to leave a plot of uncultivated land so that the wild grasses, even weeds, could grow there, for "they too proclaim the beauty of the Father of all beings." He further asked that in the gardens where the friars raised vegetables that one part be set aside for planting flowers and fragrant herbs "so that all who contemplate them may be drawn to eternal sweetness." (SF)

Our present-day culture finds in Francis a great deal of that for which we hunger and thirst. The expansion of the dimension of the anima in terms of gentleness, care, and living together answers a collective demand of our age in agony. A clear path is left where Francis directed his attention, a path strewn with affection, enthusiasm, and tremendous goodness toward all creatures, especially toward the disinherited of society. For Francis, the small happiness of our troubled existence sinks its roots in the heart of the Father of infinite goodness, but also in a human heart capable of compassion and emotion. Nourished by these two roots, existence is made happy with a finite joy, foretasting already what the Father has prepared for all in his kingdom. If we do not approach the Father, life becomes empty and existence insupportable. If we do not give ear to the heart and its needs, everything remains sterile and dark. Without the Father, the heart remains barren. Without the heart, the Father has no warmth. (SF)

Mystery of Iniquity

The crosses on which the lowly and defenseless are put to death as martyrs ought to be denounced and condemned, for God detests them. (CPCH)

Every human is oppressor and oppressed alike, both graced and ungraced. No one is so much the oppressor as to be beyond liberating grace. No one is so graced as not to be a bearer of oppressive sin. (LG)

Totalitarian regimes characteristically stamp out their bloody past and conceal the deaths and exterminations, because death by violence bears within it God's own cry: Where is your brother? This cry leads to a bad conscience and gnaws at the conscience of the powerful like a worm. It is stubborn, and it is always making itself heard. (TCL)

We even say, "People in the shantytowns are poor but they're happy. Better to be poor and happy than to be wealthy and utterly miserable." All we are doing is tranquilizing our conscience, but we do not help fill the plate of someone in the shantytown, nor will their children no longer suffer brain deficiency due to anemia and malnourishment. We are sidestepping the human iniquity involved in material poverty. In the Bible the poor person means the one who is indigent, bent over, weak, in misery, or condemned to penury. The Bible views such poverty as an evil that humiliates the human being and offends God. Human beings were made lord over the earth, not its slave; they were created in the image and likeness of God. To offend that image is to offend God, its author. (TCL)

I don't think violence is the answer for Latin America ... The great challenge facing the various social groups that want to make changes, and the church, which has made an option for transforming society, is to make an option for the people, to work with the people, and to reestablish that minimum of social cohesion and awareness as a people without which any revolution will fail. (*Diário de Pernambuco*, October 1978)

Evil has never been experienced in a vague, abstract form, nor have grace and goodness. We are always dealing with concrete situations, whether favorable or unfavorable, with the destructive or constructive historical forces of human relationships, of decent, comradely relationships, with ideologies of power and domination, or with those of cooperation and participation, with concrete bearers in the form of groups or of persons who embody these ideologies in their practical social life. Evil has a definite physiognomy, even though it may be concealed behind masks and disguises. (LP)

The problem of evil is a problem not of theodicy but of ethics. Evil — its burden and its defeat — is understood not by speculating about it, but by taking up a practice of combat for good, by embracing those causes that produce love and deliverance from the crosses of the world ... The cross is not there to be understood. It is there to be taken up —

to be carried in the footsteps of the Son of Man, who took up his cross and by that cross accomplished our redemption. (PCPW)

There may be a thousand fingers pointed at us in condemnation, destroying our honor, besmirching our intentions, dismissing what we do, but if our conscience does not condemn us, actually no one has condemned us. (VSR)

God does not explain why there is suffering—God suffers alongside us. God does not explain why there is sorrow—God became the man of sorrows. God does not explain why there is humiliation—God empties himself. We are no longer alone in our vast loneliness. God is with us. We are no longer in solitude, but rather in solidarity. The arguments from reason are silenced. It is the heart that speaks. It tells the story of a God who became a child, who does not ask questions but who acts, who does not offer explanations but lives out an answer. (EHJ)

There are times in life when the Christian conscience must denounce sin that betrays the truth of human beings and of Christ. Living in the midst of the world, Christians are called to bear witness to the sacred mystery of humanity that was assumed by God and to defend the divine right that is identified with the inviolable right of every human being to be respected as a person. To keep silent in the face of injustices and violations of the sacredness of every human being (res sacra homo) is to be an accomplice. Of course, it is easy and convenient. All sorts of reasons are invoked to justify absenteeism on our part: the need for good order, discipline, (false) unity, and noninvolvement in political questions, for example. But the grace of God leads us to brave danger, to assume the consequences of boldness, to overcome inhibiting fear, and to speak out boldly. (LG)

Based on the paschal mystery of Jesus, Christianity speaks of suffering only in terms of victory over it. It speaks of death now that it has been overcome through resurrection. We no longer stand in the situation of the rebellious Job with no answers for the myriad questions prompted by pain and suffering. There is a final answer: now that death has been defeated, we can be calm and resigned in accepting death, for it is no longer the scarecrow that had us frightened. It is our transit to the Father. (VSR)

From the time of Job, reason has always been challenged to reconcile the existence of a God of love with the evil found in the world. No matter how much such geniuses as St. Augustine or Leibniz contrive arguments to exonerate God and explain suffering, the suffering does not disappear. Understanding suffering no more does away with suffering than listening to recipes assuages hunger. (LP)

Each generation has its own "evil one" against which it must particularly protect itself and because of which it must implore divine protection. This evil being embodies the widespread wickedness that permeates humanity. In our own time, the evil one who offends God and debases human persons appears in the form of a collective selfishness embodied in an elitist, exclusivist social system that has no solidarity with the great multitudes of the poor. He has a name; he is the capitalism of private property and the capitalism of the state. In the name of money, privileges, and the reinforcement of governmental structures he holds men and women in terror. Many of them are imprisoned, tortured, and killed . . . This evil one has his ways of tempting; he slyly creeps into our minds and makes the heart insensitive to those structural inequities that he has created. (LP)

In Jesus' resurrection God has shown that he sides with the crucified of history. The executioner shall not triumph over his victim. God has raised the victim, and thereby our thirst for a world of ultimate justice, a world of a communion of sisters and brothers at the last, is not cheated. "Insurrection" against injustice confers a new meaning on *Resurrection*. Those who "rise up" to do battle for justice will rise up to new life as well. (FE)

Freedom and Liberation

Human freedom is not a lighthearted child's game. It is a risk and a mystery entailing absolute frustration in hatred or radical attainment in love. Freedom makes everything possible: not only heaven but also hell. (VAM)

Total liberation, generated by full freedom, constitutes the essence of the reign of the eschatological goodness of God. History is en route to this goal. Our task is to hasten that process. God's reign has an essentially future dimension that is unattainable by human practices; it is the object of eschatological hope. (FE)

The complete liberation proposed by God traverses the route of partial liberations; these are not its cause, but they anticipate, and prepare for, complete liberation. Thus the human being is never a mere spectator, nor is God simply a benefactor. (FE)

The historical Jesus refused to countenance the imposition of God's will by force. This would have excused human beings from their own task of liberation: they would no longer have been the agents of their own personal and social transformation, but merely its beneficiaries. Jesus preferred death to the imposition of God's reign by means of violence. Otherwise, what arose would not be God's reign but a realm created by the will of human power, a reign based on subjugation and the privation of freedom. (FE)

Christians are generally not hated for calling themselves Christians. They are persecuted and hated for being committed to a liberation process and for claiming that this commitment arises out of living the gospel and from prayer. (IFP)

We live not in the world we desire but in the one forced upon us. We do not do everything we want, but only that which we can and are allowed to do. Only an idealistic vision of history and of the individual conceives of freedom as pure spontaneity and creativity. Freedom is attained within a circumscribed area, and extending it always involves an onerous liberation process. It is a sign of maturity to accept with serenity and inner detachment those things that, objectively speaking, we cannot change. Even in situations of this sort we can exercise our freedom in the way we assume and integrate into our personal life journey the dictates of history. For this we need *amor fati*, as the ancients called it, love for what is unavoidable, embracing it with neither bitterness nor serenity. (SF)

Liberation depends on the degree of oppression. Oppression in Africa is of one kind, reflected in a cultural order in which white colonizing cultures have destroyed the cultural world of Africans. In that context liberation theology strives to defend black culture. In Latin America oppression is more economic, political, and cultural, and is made manifest in the impoverishment of the vast masses of the population. In Europe oppression is personal in nature: loneliness, helplessness, life without meaning, and well-off populations who live in the luxurious enjoyment of the goods they produce and pile up by exploiting the Third World. For each of these oppressions there are different kinds of liberations. It is important to interrelate these liberations so that they do not conflict with one another. (*Mundo Jovem*, April 1985)

Perfect joy or perfect freedom derives from a love so intense that it not only puts up with, but even loves and happily embraces what is negative. Those who have internalized such a practice of love are the only ones who are truly free, for nothing can threaten them: if they are raised up to heaven their attitude is not changed by vanity; likewise, if they are thrust into the depths of hell, their attitude is not altered by bitterness. They are completely self-possessed and thus beyond the reach of good or evil. The splendor of this conquest shines forth in permanent and unshakable joy. In the course of his life Francis had attained such freedom; that is why he was called "the ever-joyful" brother. (SF)

Only human beings dream in their sleeping and waking hours of new worlds where interpersonal relationships will be ever-more equitable — a new heaven and a new earth. Only the human person creates utopias. These utopias are not mere escape mechanisms by which the contradictions of the present are avoided. They are part of human life, because human beings continually project, plan the future, live on promises, and are nourished on hope. These are the utopias that keep the absurd from taking charge of history. (LP)

Rights of the Poor,
Rights of God

As God is the God of life, so it is that God generates life. And so God succors and defends those whose lives are threatened, or who share less in the gift of life. This is why God is, in a special way, the God of the poor. The rights of the poor are rights that regard life itself, rights calculated to maintain and expand life. Therefore the rights of the poor are rights of God. (WTLP)

The option for the poor entails an option against poverty because it is unjust and inhumane. It is an option for justice and for liberation from a situation that causes people to die too soon, to die before their time. The alternative to poverty is not wealth but justice, and relationships of fellowship. Poverty and wealth are expressions of a sick and dehumanized society. (*Témoinage Chrétien* [France], December 1986)

What space does our society create so the poor can meet, state their problems, hear their own voice, and find acceptance in their own culture? The only time they speak in public is when they are summoned to the police station to give testimony, or in front of a judge to make some kind of statement, or to the school teacher to give an account of their children. They do not speak on their own behalf; their voice is always an echo of someone else's voice, that of their masters. (TEP)

Neither the state with all its paternalism, nor the churches with their aid programs, nor the emotional charity by some of the privileged are going to resolve the problems of the poor. It is the poor themselves who will do so. The poor should not be defined simply as those who do not have. The poor *do* have some things: creativity, power to resist, survival skills, and the historic power to change society when they manage to get organized and create their own means of struggle. Only the poor liberate the poor. What the churches and other social classes can do is become involved in the struggle of the poor. (FE)

When the starting point is the rich, the poor can only be seen as the needy, those who do not have. Only a vision of the poor whose starting point is the poor themselves can enable them to discover their power, their dignity, and their own human wealth. From the first angle, the poor are at best an object of aid; from the second, they are agents capable of bringing about change. The first kind of relationship is charitable; the second, liberating. (FE)

The resurrected Jesus is present and active in a special way in those who in the vast ambit of history and life carry forward his cause. This is independent of their ideological colorings or adhesion to some religion or Christian belief. Wherever people seek the good, justice, humanitarian love, solidarity, communion, and understanding between people, wherever they dedicate themselves to overcoming their own egoism, making this world more human and fraternal, and opening themselves to the normative transcendent for their

lives, there we can say, with all certainty, that the resurrected one is present, because the cause for which he lived,
suffered, was tried, and executed is being carried forward.
"Whoever is not against us, is with us." (JCL)

We sanctify the name of God when by our own life, by our own actions of solidarity, we help to build more peaceful and more just human relationships, cutting off access to violence and one person's exploitation of another. God is always offended when violence is done to a human being, made in the divine image and likeness. And God is always sanctified when human dignity is restored to the dispossessed and the victims of violence. (LP)

What is most annoying to the dominant classes and to those agencies of social control and information is to have heard Christians say that their option for the impoverished has not come from reading Marx (*et consortes*), but from prayer, meditation on the Word of God, and following the practice of Jesus. (FE)

A person is not just interested in deadening hunger and surviving "somehow." Eating means more than a mere satisfaction of nutritional requirements; it is a communitarian act and a communion rite. Eating is not as enjoyable or fully human if done in sight of the misery of others, the Lazaruses at the foot of the table, waiting for the leftover crumbs. Daily bread provides a basic and necessary happiness for life. If there is to be any happiness, it must be communicated and shared. That is how it is with bread: it is *human* bread to the extent that it is shared and supports a bond of communion. Then happiness is found, and human hunger is satisfied. (LP)

Liberation Theology
and
Faith's Political Dimension

The European study of liberation begins with the "topic" as such. Liberation is a fundamental concept in biblical theology and in the tradition of emancipation found in modern culture. When dealing with it theologically, the theologian researches scripture, tradition, the teachings of the church, and the recent opinion of theologians. The idea is to systematically reconstruct the idea of liberation and to establish a critical grounding for the topic; once this is done, its consequences for the everyday life of the faithful are deduced, and advice and instructions for future action are drawn up.

The Latin American and Third World perspective starts from the opposite pole. First it examines the concrete practice of the oppressed, their progress and their allies; it asks about the participation of individual Christians, base communities and sectors of the church in the overall liberation process. Then it asks a number of questions. What is the relationship of this journey and this practice to the unfolding of God's plan? To what extent is this process an incipient and historical realization of the kingdom of God, which is a kingdom of justice, of fellowship and of peace? What relationship is there between this concrete liberation and salvation in Jesus Christ who, when he was among us, surely made an option for the poor, cured the sick, and liberated the oppressed? Finally, it offers a critical evaluation, in the light of faith, of the presence of Christians and the practice of non-Christians as well, and calls for concrete actions aimed at furthering the struggle for liberation ... It is this perspective that constitutes the originality of the theology of liberation, and that distinguishes it from other theologies *on* liberation. (LADOC, January-February 1985)

Liberation theology ponders not a theory, but the gross and bloodstained fact of severe poverty, oppression, and premature death. If liberation theology is to move beyond naivety and being morally scandalized and crying out in prophetic protest to become an organized rational body of thought, it must make use of analytical tools that can serve to decode the mechanisms that cause this iniquity. The collective poverty of the masses did not fall down from heaven, it was not brought about by nature, and it is not innocent. It is the product of economic, political, and social mechanisms. Pronouncing a moral judgment, saying it is a social sin while remaining in the realm of ethics is not enough. These things carry an image of God, they manipulate the figure and message of Jesus Christ, and they produce a political theology to justify the way things are. Theology's role is not simply that of unmasking how faith is being perverted, but of developing in a positive sense, or recovering, the true countenance of the God of life and the genuine message of Jesus, which liberates from all oppressions. (*Jornal do Brasil*, August 1984)

Theology either thinks critically about reality and is liberating, or it ceases to be theology and takes its place among the ideological forces sustaining the status quo, which is mistakenly regarded as the most just and most equitable. (LG)

Liberation theology's greatness lies in the fact that it experiences the very problems our people are experiencing and suffering just as they do. Even if this theology should be condemned, the people would not stop struggling. The process of liberation will continue and will require a Christian reflection, since many Christians are involved in that process. We theologians have to reflect on the meaning of this process in God's eyes and in the light of God's design in history. God is already present in this historic process; the task of theology is to read the signs of God's reign in all this. (*Fôlha de São Paulo*, October 1984)

The theologian of liberation opts to see social reality from a point of departure in the reality of the poor—opts to analyze processes in the interests of the poor, and to act for liberation in concert with the poor. This is a *political* decision, for it defines the theologian as a social agent, occupying a determined place in a correlation of social forces: a place on the side of the poor and oppressed. At the same time it is an *ethical* option, because it rejects the status quo. It refuses to accept the situation as it is and experiences ethical indignation at the scandal of poverty and exploitation. It evinces an interest in the advancement of the poor, which can occur only in the presence of structural change in historico-social reality. Finally, it is an *evangelical* definition: in the gospels, the poor are the primary addressees of Jesus' message and constitute the eschatological criterion by which the salvation or perdition of every human being is determined (Mt 25:35–46). (SAL)

Liberation theology also has in mind helping church institutions liberate themselves from modes of life, ideas, and practices related to the past, which are not always appropriate to the new situation of the church's pastoral work among the poor. Thus liberation theology calls for a society that is democratic, oriented to the poor majority, pluralistic, and open. The church in such a society must be appropriate, one that is likewise open and pluralistic, where being the people of God means more than attending a parish: it means participating in the life of the community, being educated to be an agent of liberation, and not reproducing the prevailing system. (*O Globo*, April 1986)

Our overall option is clear: our real concern is not liberation theology but the liberation of our peoples in history. Liberation theology must serve that liberation. (TCL)

For Christians faith is not one tool among several for human liberation. No, it is much more: it is the entry into, and emergence from, all struggle, the larger horizon within which everything is situated and everything is transfigured from a perspective of eternity. Christians are restoring to faith its dignity. The purpose of faith is neither to hide the evils of society nor to relieve the oppressors of their bad conscience, but to produce the fruits of the reign of God, which are truth, justice, and a common life in a family spirit. (IFP)

What sustains the commitment of Christians to the humiliated and injured of this world is not only critical analysis of the situation or the compelling force of their theological treatment of that social analysis, but also a practice and mystique of solidarity and of being identified with the oppressed. It is this powerful mystique that nourishes service to one's brothers and sisters as service given to God. Passion for God is connected to passion for the people. (FE)

Every christology is relevant to its particular social and historical circumstances. In other words, a christology is always engaged and committed . . . The real question, then, is not *whether* a particular kind of christology is partisan or engaged, but *to whom and to what* this particular kind of christology is committed and engaged. What cause does it serve? The christology that proclaims Jesus Christ as Lib-erator commits itself to the economic, social, and political liberation of the oppressed and dominated groups of society. It takes as theologically relevant the historical liberation of the vast masses of our continent, and it says, this is what christology ought to think, and in praxis this is the path it ought to encourage. In other words, liberation christology seeks to compose and articulate its content and style in a manner calculated to bring out the liberation dimensions of the historical Jesus' life. (FE)

If participation, reconciliation, harmony, and peace are not vibrant in the church; if there is no respect for the dignity of each believer; if tolerance and comprehension for diver-sity and difference among its members is lacking, then the church's appeal for reconciliation between people, peace among nations and unity between legitimate pluralisms becomes an innocuous bit of ecclesiastical jargon and a countersign leading people to curse God and to find plenty of reasons for failing to see the credibility of Christianity. (DHM)

As Christians pursue liberation from immense social evil, they must develop alongside the perennially valid personal virtues of a political holiness: to love in the midst of class conflicts, to hope for fruits that will come only in the far distant future, to stand in solidarity with oppressed groups, to ascetically submit to decisions taken in community and, finally, to be ready to give their own life in fidelity to the gospel and to their oppressed brothers and sisters. (IFP)

We have to be cruel and at odds with our own humanity if we seek to sidestep the problem with the facile argument that the church must not be a political tool. The crucial question is: A tool for what kind of politics? There is a politics of justice and solidarity with the unimportant and the slaughtered. If we do not have that justice, all our purist attitudes about maintaining Christian identity are not worth much. A formal identity, one of keeping our hands clean out of fear of getting mixed up in the grime of history, is unworthy of Jesus Christ who was able to take the side of the poor and was not afraid of being persecuted, regarded as one who denied God, and being cursed and reviled on the cross. (TEP)

To claim that economics is unrelated to ethics and that politics is neutral is tantamount to losing the perspective of faith. Nothing is neutral before God: it serves either for human liberation or for perdition. (TCL)

The progress made by liberation theology is irreversible, because it is a practice, a process that is historic, real, and concrete, and comes from those who bear the promise and hope of a more humane society. (Fôlha de São Paulo, October 1984)

Ecology and Spirituality

An ecological culture is slowly taking shape all around the world. Even back in the 1970s one could observe that significant groups were moving toward an option for voluntary simplicity, which entailed giving up consumerism and breaking away from a purely utilitarian logic. People are coming to regard themselves as postmaterialist and as sensitive to spiritual issues. A logic of reverence and an ethic of otherness is emerging.

All beings within nature deserve respect; they all have their identity. They are an otherness that puts limits to the human being's will to dominate. Hence we can rightly speak of an ecological justice — that is, of a just relationship with the beings in creation — for they are all around us, and in some sense they are also citizens. Thus arises a spirituality in which the human city is human not simply by the fact that it is made up of persons and institutions; plants, the waters, the pure air, the animals, and healthy conditions of material life are also to be brought together in harmony.

Some groups go deeper into the issue of an ethic of reverence: What underlies this spirituality and what values does it entail? May it not be that there is something unifying the whole of nature, making it cosmos (harmony) rather than chaos, and so that from chaos new forms of life are ever emerging?

The modern conception of the world, worked out on the basis of Bohr's quantum physics, Einstein's theory of relativity, and Heisenberg's uncertainty principle, suggests that

the world should be represented as a complex combination
of energies. Deep down, everything is energy. Matter itself
is a moment of crystalized energy. The universe of energies
is constituted by a web of relationships. All things, even
subatomic particles, exist for, with, and through one
another. Nothing exists outside relationship. To exist is to
be in relation. Some convincingly assert that everything is
manifestation of life, since life is energy relating to itself
internally. This life has myriad forms, from the primal move-

ment of original matter to the self-conscious expression of the human being.

Christian tradition has a category for understanding reality as energy and as life — the figure of the Holy Spirit. The Spirit is the creator par excellence, acts in everything that moves, makes life expand, sets the prophets, poets, charismatic leaders, and all of us on fire with enthusiasm.

The Spirit dwells in its creation similarly to the way the eternal Son dwells in the humanity of Jesus.

Christians do not find it hard to understand the incarnation through which God becomes human and lives with human destiny, but they are not very alert to the indwelling of the Spirit in creation. If they were, they would have a spirituality that was spontaneous, cosmic, and connected to life. In embracing the world, we embrace God. Long ago a mystic who lived and felt the indwelling of the Spirit in the world rightly observed:

The spirit sleeps in the rock, dreams in the flower, feels in animals, knows what it feels in men, and feels what it knows in women.

There is here a deep intuition of the cosmic omnipresence of the Spirit. It is not limited to Christians. We find similar thoughts in Zen Buddhist mystics, in Native Americans (like the Sioux in the North and the Bororo in the South), and in contemporary religious thinkers.

Visions like these help us nourish our ecological mystique. We are immersed in an ocean of life, pulsation, and communion. We constitute a whole in the Spirit, who permeates the entire cosmos and us as well. We are, all of us, the snail on the pathway and the stars in the heavens, truly brothers and sisters. (*Frente Popular*, June 1991)

Christmas:
The Eternal Child
within Us

Christmas is far more than just a celebration in the Christian calendar. It is a universal celebration of the human heart, of pure and simple faith. Of this much our faith reassures us: we need not be afraid of God. God is a child, whose gentle sobs do not frighten anyone away, and whose arms are swathed and unthreatening. More than Lord of hosts and the All-powerful who creates or destroys everything, God is tenderness and humaneness. God does not just want to visit us — God decides to dwell with us — to have skin, senses, feelings, heart, joy, and longing. That is why Christmas is the feast of reconciliation with one of the deepest desires of the human being: that of feeling utterly accepted, of not being threatened by anyone, of finding God's warm heart.

Christmas is also the celebration of a very human faith becoming hope. Faith-hope lies in this: it is not self-seeking profit, conflict, and the harsh struggle for life that have the last word, but rather tenderness, gratuity, play, good will, and love. In this sense, the child lying between the ox and the ass in the manger does not represent the beginning of life. He is its symbol and its fullness. Faith-hope assures us that despite all the layers of ashes we accumulate over our heart, it can always keep beating. It retains an original innocence. In it there dwells a child; once we were — and indeed we never cease to be — that child.

Actually, however, the kind of life to which we subject ourselves, at least for the last five hundred years in what is

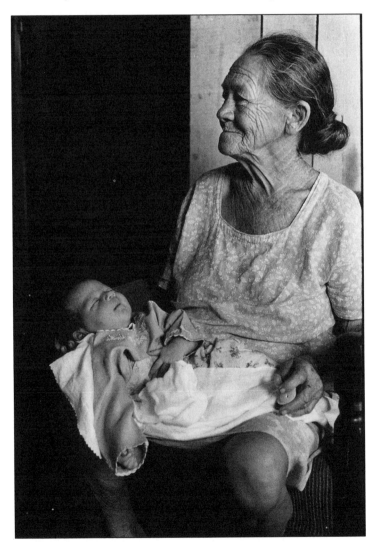

touted as modernity, leads us to run around from one place
to another, to do everything in a hurry, to break all natural
rhythms, of day and night, near and far, and so we often
feel aged. The child that is us, who can take its time con-
versing with family or friends, who can combine seriousness
with joking, work with leisure, and the gratuitous with duty,
withdraws into the depths of our heart — and there begins
to live off dreams. But these dreams are part of what is most
serious about us. The child inside us dreams of a reconciled
world, of an atmosphere of celebration, where people are
all friends. That child dreams, as did the prophet Isaiah
almost three thousand years ago: the wolf will lie down with
the lamb, the lion and the ox will eat together, and the
child will have no fear of playing by the serpent's den. In
contemporary terms, the child dreams of cities without
slums, of people living together without violence, of our
forests being respected, of Indians defended, of women liberated, of blacks free of discrimination.

What would happen to us if we were unable to dream?
We would be smothered in the brutality of everyday facts.
We would remain enmeshed in the things we build, which
are always limited. Dreaming frees us forward and upward.
It does away with the fatalism of our history, for that history
can always be different. Miracles are possible. Magic exists.
Is there any magic greater than this: Jesus being God incar-
nate in the form of a child in the manger?

At Christmas for one moment, for one night, we can
glimpse the truth of the dream. People sit around the table
and celebrate the supper. It is full communion, with people,
lights, meals, presents. On this holy night for a moment we
feel that we are important for somebody; we are not a
nobody. We exchange presents as an expression of friendship, affection, and the child dwelling within us is born, and
today stands at the center of life. Because of the Christmas
child, we regain the courage to live, despite all the oppres-

sions weighing down upon our life or overburdening our conscience. It is good to be human, to be men and women, and to have to build our own humanity every day. Because of the child slumbering in us we are convinced that the light is more justified than the darkness; and that light gives us every reason to go on with our life and our struggle. (*O Tatui*, December 1990)

God — The Poor — Liberation

Speech given November 26, 1990, upon receiving an honorary doctorate in political science from the University of Turin (Italy).

Ladies and gentlemen:

I find moments like this deeply moving. They take me back far away from here and a long time ago. I cannot help but recall my childhood. My parents' house in southern Brazil comes back to me. Back then in the 1930s my parents had come to the far south of Brazil. They were themselves children of Italian immigrants who had come from northern Italy, from Feltre, Seren del Grappa, and Belluno. Their children — in other words, my parents — colonized new regions of forests and mountains, and fertile valleys where the only people were Guarani Indians. They went into those woods, and created settlements, where only Italian was spoken. When they cleared areas, the first thing built after their own houses was a little church and a school. Everything was made of wood, and quite simple.

My father taught school, led prayers in the chapel, served as a druggist, assisted at births, and was a justice of the peace. By night he taught a course in Portuguese for the older people who spoke only Italian at home. As the eldest in a family of eleven children, I followed my father everywhere. I got to go along to the mill, taking our wheat or corn to be ground into flour. In the cold of our harsh winter, in freezing mornings, sometimes with frost on the ground, it was hard to get up early and go three or four hours on horseback to the nearest mill.

My mother was illiterate, but she had a lot of common sense. While my father was teaching morning, afternoon, and evening, she was working in the field, taking care of the chickens, pigs, and cattle, and providing for our house, which was full of children.

That barefoot child from a poor Italian immigrant family that was hardworking and striving to get ahead is the same person who is speaking to you today and accepting this degree from the Università degli Studi di Torino. I am very pleased to be able to pay tribute to my parents and my family. It was not God's will that they live long enough to savor this moment. But where they are, I know that they are present in everything. And with the joyful Venetian spirit they must also be happy and feel fulfilled.

Ladies and gentlemen, I have come from the stone age. For that was how rough our situation was fifty years ago in the area where I was born. I have come a long way. I had to rise step by step through various phases of human development. Only when I was ten years old did I learn Portuguese, the language of my country, Brazil, since at home we spoke only Venetian dialect. Later in elementary and high school, I learned Latin and Greek, and then philosophy and theology. Finally I got my doctorate at the University of Munich. Immediately afterward, I became involved in pastoral work with the people, among the poor, and discovered the perverse logic of the dependent capitalism, which makes most people poor. Then came the development of liberation theology, and my tribulations with doctrinal authorities in the church. All of this involved a great deal of suffering and struggle. I also want to make sure to mention my modest joy at having participated in the working out of a new way of being a church at the grassroots among the poor, and sharing at least a little in the passion of my people.

Why am I recalling all of this right now? Because in my view this degree is not being conferred primarily on me because of my own life. Our purpose here is to honor a cause and celebrate a struggle by millions of Christians on my continent who have helped in the formulation of my thinking. I do not want to overlook the anonymous people alongside whom I have been able to journey, those who have sustained me with their human quality and their faith. I single out the people of the community of San João Batista in Petrópolis where I live and work, a huge shantytown, which makes its living by salvaging things from garbage. I share in the life of the community, in its struggles and hopes. I know so many people throughout the vastness of Brazil, men and women, who are oppressed by a dehumanizing system, who find meaning in life, and day by day renew their hope by participating in Christian base communities, popular movements and land struggles, defending native people, and protecting the Amazon forest. Among them are confessors, masters of wisdom, and martyrs.

I have known so many Italians in the shantytowns of Rio, São Paulo, and Recife and in the heart of the Amazon jungle in Acre who are completely dedicated to the poor and risk their lives in the process of humanization and liberation of those who are least on earth. They have left their beautiful country, given up its culture, and they have cut short their own lives; they have been exposed to a thousand dangers and yet have not dulled their sensitivity or lost their gentleness. They are fellow travelers along the road, and very often they teach me.

In the name of all them I accept the degree with which this university wants to honor the just cause of all of them, the dignity of their struggle, and the holiness of their destiny. I make my own the experience of one of our greatest poets, Pablo Neruda: "It is both unforgettable and ravaging to incarnate even for a moment, the struggle of the oppressed." At this moment it is I who am here, but I am thinking of all of them. Many of them could be standing here in my place, more deservedly than I.

In the name of all of them, men and women, people who in the words of Revelation are coming from the great tribulation of life, people who are poor and outcast, oppressed classes, humiliated races, silenced cultures: in the name of all of them, I say to you: Thank you very much!

Someone a bit puzzled, might ask, *come mai?* – How is it that a theologian is being given an honorary doctorate in the history of political thought? Such a thing becomes comprehensible if we come to understand the core of liberation theology, for it has developed a theology of the political and likewise a political theology on behalf of the vast poor majority in the Third World.

What is specific about liberation theology lies not in the fact that, like all theologies, it speaks of God, Christ, the Spirit, the church, the human being, grace, sin, and politics. The crucial point is that we speak about all these things from the situation of the poor.

The poor are at the heart of liberation theology. When we speak of the poor, we understand them as something collective and conflictive. As I just said, they are outcast groups, whole classes that are oppressed, cultures that have been broken down and are treated with contempt, like those of our Indians, women suffering discrimination, and others who suffer repression because of race, sex, or disease. These collective negative realities are conflictive because they are the result of unjust relations, and because they represent a cry of protest and call for historic transformation.

The poor as a group and in conflict are our starting point for posing the issues of God, Christ, the Spirit, the church, politics, and other theological questions. If we start with the poor, our God is revealed as the God of life because it is the God who hears the moaning of captives as they yearn for life and freedom. If we start with the poor, Jesus Christ is seen to be the one who brings complete liberation, who sets liberation in motion by overcoming illness and death, and by arousing the hope of the poor when he says to them, "Blessed are you poor, for yours is the justice of the reign." If we start with the poor, the Holy Spirit emerges as the one who provides the oppressed with strength to resist and continually arouses in them dreams and practices aiming at changing this world. If we start with the poor, it becomes clear that the church should always make a preferential option for the poor and regard them as the primary object of its pastoral concern. If we start with the poor as a group and in conflict, we can see how important it is that politics always be guided by the objective interests of the majority, and hence how politics should be both transforming and democratic.

Clearly, the poor are not just one topic on the theological agenda alongside others. They are not an entry in a theological dictionary. They are the horizon within which we read and interpret other issues. Hence the poor are far more than a topic for theological and political reflection. The poor constitute an important social and epistemological locus or source.

How are we to speak of God from within the shantytowns, except by speaking of the God of life? How are we to speak of Jesus Christ starting with the native peoples of the Peruvian highlands who have been subjugated for five centuries, except by speaking of Jesus Christ the liberator? How are we to think of the church from the standpoint of women who have always suffered discrimination in a male culture and a celibate church, except by speaking of the church as sacrament of liberation? How are we to think of new directions for society from the standpoint of the victims of the current thrust, what is being planned in North Atlantic countries and occupies the minds of our leaders who talk about modernity and modern science and technology, without mentioning a popular social democracy?

Liberation theology has offered its collaboration in the realms of faith and politics. Allow me to explain in a few words what the poor mean in our understanding of the task of theology and as a challenge to political life.

Here is the question: *What is the importance of the poor collectively and in conflict for theology and politics?*

We are confronted with three visions: the traditional and modernizing visions, and that of liberation theology.

The traditional vision says: the poor are the have-nots. They must be aided by the haves. Consequently, since the beginning of Christianity there have been programs in the church to aid the poor, as there have been in the state. Paternalistic programs to hand things out have been set up. This approach provides benefits, but it is not participatory. The poor have no value, since they are seen from the eyes of the rich. They always remain dependent.

The modernizing vision says: the poor are a social problem. These people do have something, they have potential, but it is not being utilized. They are underdeveloped. So they have to be developed, through schooling, through training, and by being drawn into the productive process. The task of the state is to create jobs for these poor people in society.

The traditional vision sees the poor but does not see their collective nature. The modernizing vision recognizes that they are a body but fails to see that they are conflictive. However, the poor are the result of political and economic mechanisms that prize capital over labor. An unequal relationship produces social conflict. The poor are victims of this conflict. In order for them to enter into the production process, there has to be a critique of the society that is always producing and reproducing inequality and injustice.

The third position is that of liberation theology. This

position says: the poor do have potential – and not just to fill up the labor force of the present system, but to transform this system. Once they have become aware, gotten themselves organized, and established links with other allies, they can transform society in the direction of greater participa-

tion and equality. That is why the perspective of the poor is neither that of handouts nor modernization—it is liberating.

The poor help us discover the conflict in our society, conflict based on class, race, culture, and gender.

The poor help us understand the central perspective of the Judeo-Christian tradition, the ties that run: God—the poor—liberation. Certainly God is a God-mystery who dwells in light inaccessible. But this is an ethical God who hears the cry of the oppressed, whether in Egypt or in any other situation of discouragement. God leaves the inaccessible light and comes down in order to liberate the oppressed. Things are not all the same to God; God takes sides against the pharaoh and against all the oppressors in history; God takes the side of those who suffer and cry out for life. Hence there is a close and essential connection that runs: God—the poor—liberation.

This vision helps the church overcome an alliance it has made in history, its complicity with power and domination, which often in the history of the church has run: God—the powerful—submission. The church joined up with the powerful, and with them it evangelized peoples. The result is an evangelization along the lines of subjugation. Latin America provides an outstanding example of that.

Only by moving into the world of the poor, and making an option for the poor and the outcast, will the church grasp its mission within this sacred alliance of God—the poor—liberation. The result of this sacred alliance is that the poor become agents of liberating evangelization, and not just its object. The poor evangelize the whole church insofar as they create Christian communities and share in building a church in dialogue with cultures, and ever in solidarity with those on the bottom. It will only be a church for the poor when it is first a church of the poor—that is, when the poor feel that they are active subjects of the church and not just beneficiaries of the ecclesiastical system.

Hence the poor occupy a special place. From the poor we have a better understanding of both politics and the church. Traditional and modern theology generally do not accept this place, because of the kind of thinking that prevails in universities and in industrialized societies. Liberation theology is devoted to defending the place of the poor, as a place that is specifically theirs, and is fruitful for understanding better the world, our society, the kind of development we want, the future of humankind, the mission of the churches, and the very nature of divinity.

Most of those who criticize us interpret us on the basis of the traditional handout vision or the modernizing vision. We have to struggle to explain our own specific vision, which starts from the poor and is therefore liberating. The degree I am today receiving in the name of so many others shows that we can be understood and supported.

I am very deeply convinced that there will be no solution to the question of a new relationship between North and South, for the great European family, and for worldwide conflict, if the solution does not take into account the dire poverty of two-thirds of the human race. With the end of the Cold War and the overthrow of what was called socialism, the poor of the world today stand right at the center of things. The liberation church and its liberation theology are offering their admittedly modest collaboration to this challenge facing all realms of knowledge, all organizations, all governments, and all those who have become aware of the issue. I am happy that the department of political science of the Università degli Studi di Torino has always been aware of this set of issues and has proven it by honoring me with this degree. Thank you very much.

Letter to My Companions on the Journey of Hope

There are moments in a person's life when, in order to be faithful to himself, he must change. I have changed. Not the battle itself, but the trenches from which I shall fight.

I am leaving the priestly ministry but not the church. I am leaving the Franciscan Order but not putting aside the tender and fraternal dream of St. Francis of Assisi. I continue to be and will always be a theologian in the Catholic and ecumenical mold, fighting with the poor against their poverty and in favor of their liberation. I wish to outline to my companions on this journey the reasons which brought me to this decision.

Let me begin by saying: I am leaving the Franciscan Order to maintain my freedom and in order to continue with a work in which I was being severely hampered. This work has been the reason for the fight I have put up over the last twenty-five years. To be unfaithful to what gives sense to one's life is to lose one's dignity and to diminish one's identity. This I will not do, nor do I think that God wants this of me.

The words of José Marti, a notable Cuban thinker of last century, come to mind: "It is not possible for God to put thoughts into someone's head and for a bishop, who is not God, to forbid him to express them."

But let us take a look at my journey. Since the seventies, together with other Christians, I have tried to link the gos-

pel with social injustice and the cry of the oppressed with
the God of life. From this sprang liberation theology, the
first Latin American theology with a universal relevance.
Through it we tried to rediscover the liberating power of
the Christian faith and to make concrete the "dangerous
memory" of Jesus, breaking that iron circle that has held
Latin American Christianity captive to the interests of the
powerful.

This endeavor brought us to the school of the poor and
the marginalized. We were evangelized by them. We became
more human and sensitive to their suffering. We also understood better the processes which constantly renew their suffering. From sacred anger we progressed to solidarity and
committed reflection.

We endured together with them the calumny of those
social sectors which find in traditional Christianity an ally
in maintaining their privileges, on the pretext of preserving
that order which is pure and simple disorder for the majority.
We suffer at being accused by our brothers in faith of heresy
and of collusion with Marxism. We suffer at seeing the
bonds of brotherhood publicly broken.

I have always maintained that a church is only truly at
one with the liberation of the oppressed when it itself, in
its internal life, rises above structures and practices which
imply discrimination against women, the diminishing of the
laity, the distrust of modern freedoms and the spirit of
democracy and the excessive concentration of power in the
hands of the clergy.

I have frequently made the following reflection which I
repeat here. That which is wrong in the doctrine on the
Trinity cannot be truth in the doctrine on the church. One
is taught that in the Trinity there can be no hierarchy.
Therefore, all subordination is heretical.

The divine persons are of equal dignity, of equal goodness
and power. The intimate nature of the Trinity is not soli-

tude, but communion. The interrelationship (perichoresis) of life and love interlaces the three divine persons so radically that we do not have three gods but one God-communion. But it is said of the church that it is essentially hierarchical and that the division between clerics and laity is of divine institution.

We are not against a hierarchy. But if there be hierarchy, because this can be a legitimate cultural necessity, it must always be, according to sound theological reasoning, a hierarchy of service. If it is not so, how can we truly affirm that the church is the icon of the Trinity? Where is Jesus' dream of a community of brothers and sisters if there are so many who present themselves as fathers and masters when Jesus says explicitly that we have only one father and one master (Matthew 23:8-9)?

The present way in which the church is organized (it was not always thus in history) creates and reproduces inequalities rather than bringing about the fraternal and egalitarian utopia of Jesus and the apostles.

For such views, which are moreover part of the prophetic tradition of Christianity and of the mind-set of the reformers, beginning with St. Francis of Assisi, I came under the strict vigilance of the doctrinal authorities of the Vatican. Directly or through intermediary authorities, this vigilance became like an ever-tightening tourniquet rendering my work as a theologian, teacher, lecturer, adviser, and writer almost impossible.

From 1971 onward, I have frequently received letters, warnings, restrictions and punishments.

It cannot be said that I did not cooperate. I answered all the letters. Twice, I negotiated my temporary removal from my chair of theology. I faced the "dialogue" in Rome before the Roman Catholic Church's highest doctrinal authority in 1984. I accepted the text condemning several of my opinions in 1985. And then (contrary to the sense of canon law, since I had submitted to everything) a period of "respectful silence" was imposed upon me.

I accepted this, saying: "I prefer to walk with the church (of the poor and the ecclesial base communities) than to walk alone with my theology." I was removed from the editorship of the *Revista Eclesiastica Brasileira* and from the editorial board of the Vozes Publishing House. They imposed upon me a special set of rules outside canon law, forcing me to submit everything I wrote to two sets of advance censorship, one by the Franciscan Order and the other by the bishop whose responsibility it is to grant the imprimatur.

I accepted everything and submitted. Between 1991 and 1992, the iron circle tightened still further. I was removed from the editorship of *Vozes* magazine (the oldest cultural magazine in Brazil, dating from 1904). Censorship was imposed upon the Vozes Publishing House and all the magazines it publishes.

Censorship was once again imposed on everything I wrote, whether it be an article or a book. This censorship was vigorously applied. I also had to refrain for an unspecified length of time from the general teaching of theology.

My personal experience of dealing these last twenty years with doctrinal power is this: It is cruel and merciless. It forgets nothing, forgives nothing; it exacts a price for everything.

To achieve their end — the imprisonment of theological intelligence — the doctrinal powers take all the time necessary and use all the means necessary. They act directly or use intermediaries or force one's brethren within the Franciscan Order to exercise a function which by canon law belongs only to those who have doctrinal authority (bishops and the Congregation for the Doctrine of the Faith).

I feel as though I have come up against a brick wall. I can no longer go forward. To go back would imply the sacrificing of my personal dignity and the abandoning of the struggle of so many years.

Not all is permitted within the church. And Jesus himself died to bear witness to the fact that not everything is allowed in this world. There are limits beyond which one must not step: the rights, the dignity, and the freedom of the human person. The person who continually stoops ends up curved and thus dehumanized.

The hierarchical church does not have the monopoly of evangelical values nor is the Franciscan Order the only heir of the Sun of Assisi. Besides these, there exist the Christian community and the torrent of Franciscan fraternity and tenderness in which I will share with joy and freedom.

Before I become bitter, before I see the human bases of Christian faith and hope destroyed in me, before I see the evangelical image of God-the-communion-of-persons shaken, I prefer to change course. Not direction.

The prime motives which have inspired my life will continue unaltered: the fight for the kingdom, which begins with the poor; the passion for the gospel; compassion for the suffering; commitment to the liberation of the oppressed; the linking of the most critical thought with the most inhuman reality and the nurturing of the tenderness towards every being in creation in the light of St. Francis of Assisi's example.

I will not cease to love the mysterious and sacramental character of the church and to understand its historical limitations with lucidity and the necessary tolerance.

There is undeniably a grave crisis within the Roman Catholic Church as it stands. There are two basic attitudes in violent opposition within it. The first believes in the power of discipline and the second in the intrinsic power of the course of things. The first considers that the church needs order and, for this reason, places all the stress on obedience and submission.

This attitude is largely assumed by hegemonic sectors of the central administration of the church. The second thinks that the church must free itself and, for this reason, puts its faith in the Spirit, who ferments history and in the vital forces, which, like humus, give fecundity to the centuries-old ecclesial body. This attitude is represented by important sectors in the peripheral churches of the Third World and Brazil.

I categorically partake of the second attitude; that of those people for whom faith is the overcoming of fear, of those who have hope in the future of the defenseless flower and in the invisible roots which sustain the tree.

Brothers and sisters, companions on the journey of hope, may my action not discourage you in the struggle to build a society in which collaboration and solidarity are less difficult to realize because this is what Jesus' practice and the enthusiasm of the Spirit invite us to. Let us help the institutional church to be more evangelical, compassionate, human and committed to the liberty and liberation of the sons and daughters of God.

Let us not walk with our back to the future but with eyes wide open so that we may discern in the present the signs of a new world wanted by God and within it a new way of being the church; communal, popular, liberating the ecumenical.

For my part, I wish to involve myself through my intellectual work in the building of an Indo-Afro-American Christianity inculturated in the bodies, skins, dances, suffering, joys, and the languages of our peoples in answer to God's gospel — an answer which has not been fully given despite 500 years of Christian presence in our continent.

I shall continue in the universal priesthood of the faithful, which is also an expression of the lay Jesus' priesthood as is recorded for us by the author of the Letter to the Hebrews (7:14; 8:4).

I do not come out of this institution saddened, but calm, because I have made my own the verses of our great poet Fernando Pessoa: "Was it worth it? Everything is worth it, if the soul is not small."

I feel that, with God's grace, my soul has not been small.

United on the journey and in the grace of the one who knows the secret and destiny of all the paths we follow, I greet you with peace and all good.

LEONARDO BOFF
Rio de Janeiro,
June 28, 1992

Bibliography

Books by Leonardo Boff—1971–1991
(published by Editora Vozes, Petrópolis—unless otherwise noted)

1971
O Evangelho do Cristo Cósmico
A Oração no Mundo Secular (co-author)
Vida Religiosa e Secularização (CRB, Rio de Janeiro)

1972
Credo para Amanhã (co-author)
Jesus Cristo Libertador (Jesus Christ Liberator, Orbis Books, 1978)
A Ressurreição de Cristo—A Nossa Ressurreição na Morte
Die Kirche als Sakrament im Horizont der Welterfahrung (Paderborn)

1973
Vida para além da Morte
O Destino do Homem e do Mundo
O Espírito Santo: Pessoa, Presença, Atuação (co-author)

1974
Experimentar Deus Hoje (co-author)
A Atualidade da Experiência de Deus (CRB)
Quem é Jesus Cristo no Brasil? (co-author, ASTE)

1975
Os Sacramentos da Vida e a Vida dos Sacramentos (Sacraments of Life, Life of the Sacraments, Washington, D.C.: Pastoral Press, 1987)

131

A *Vida Religiosa e a Igreja no Processo de Libertação*
A *Mulher na Igreja, Presença e Ação* (co-author)
Pobreza, Obediencia y Realización Personal en la Vida Religiosa (Bogotá: CLAR)
Nosso Irmão Francisco de Assis (co-author)

1976
Teologia da Libertação e do Cativeiro (Lisbon: Multinova, and Petrópolis: Vozes, 1980)
A *Graça Libertadora no Mundo* (*Liberating Grace*, Orbis Books, 1979)
Encarnação: A Humanidade e a Jovialidade de Nosso Deus

1977
Paixão de Cristo—Paixão do Mundo (*Passion of Christ, Passion of the World*, Orbis Books, 1987)
Eclesiogênese (*Ecclesiogenesis: The Base Communities Reinvent the Church*, Orbis Books, 1986)
Testigos de Dios en el Corazón del Mundo (Madrid:Claretianas, *God's Witnesses in the Heart of the World*, Chicago: Claret House, 1981)

1978
A *Fe na Periferia do Mundo* (included in *Faith on the Edge*, Orbis Books, 1991)
Jesucristo y Nuestro Futuro de Liberación (Bogota: Indo-American PS)
Via-Sacra da Justiça (*Way of the Cross—Way of Justice*, Orbis Books, 1980)
Renovação Carismática Católica (co-author)

1979
O *Rostro Materno de Deus* (*The Maternal Face of God*, San Francisco: Harper & Row, 1987)
Da Libertação: O Teológico das Libertações Sócio-Históricas (co-author, *Salvation and Liberation*, Orbis Books, 1984)
O *Pai-Nosso: A Oração da Libertação Integral* (*The Lord's Prayer*, Orbis Books, 1983)

1980
A Ave-Maria: O Feminino e o Espírito Santo
Libertar para a Comunhão e Participação (CRB)
O Caminhar da Igreja com os Oprimidos (Codecri; also Vozes, 1988; in Faith on the Edge, Orbis Books, 1991)

1981
Francisco de Assis: Ternura e Vigor (Saint Francis, New York: Crossroad, 1984)
Igreja: Carisma e Poder (Church: Charism and Power, New York: Crossroad, 1985)
O Franciscanismo no Mundo de Hoje (co-author)
Pastoral Popular Libertadora (co-author, Porte Alegre)

1982
Igreja: Carisma e Poder—Da Polêmica ao Debate Teológico (co-author)
Via-Sacra da Ressurreição
Opciones de Vida: Retos al Franciscanismo (Barcelona)
Vida Segundo o Espírito
Dez Anos de Teologia (co-author, CRB)
A Igreja que Surge da Base (co-author, Paulinas)

1983
Direitos Humanos: Um Desafio à Consciência (co-author, Paulinas)
Mestre Eckhart: A Mística de Ser e de Não Ter (co-author)

1984
Teologia à Escuta do Povo
Do Lugar do Pobre (When Theology Listens to the Poor, San Francisco: Harper & Row, 1984)
Como Pregar a Cruz Hoje numa Sociedade de Crucificados

1985
Teologia da Libertação no Debate Atual (co-author; Liberation Theology: From Confrontation to Dialogue, San Francisco: Harper & Row, 1986)

Francisco de Assis: Homem do Paraíso
Roma Locuta (co-author, CDDH)

1986
Como Fazer Teologia da Libertação (co-author; *Introducing Liberation Theology*, Orbis Books and Tunbridge Wells: Burns & Oates, 1987)
E a Igreja se Fez Povo
A Trinidade, a Sociedade e a Libertação (*Trinity and Society*, Orbis Books and Tunbridge Wells: Burns & Oates, 1988)

1987
Cristãos: Como Fazer Política (co-author)
Die befreiende Botschaft (co-author, Herder)

1988
A Santíssima Trinidade é a Melhor Comunidade

1989
O Que Ficou (co-author)
Igreja, Reino de Deus e CEBs (co-author, CESEP/Paulinas)
Dor, Resistência e Esperança Cristã na América Latina (co-author, CECA/Sinodal)

1990
Fede e Perestroika (co-author, Cittadella Editrice)
Nova Evangelização: Perspectiva dos Oprimidos (*New Evangelization*, Orbis Books and Tunbridge Wells: Burns & Oates, 1991)

1991
Direitos Humanos, Direitos dos Pobres (co-author)
Francisco e a Ecologia (co-author)